RECOLLECTIONS

OF A

RELIEVING OFFICER.

I.—THE CHAIRMAN'S DAUGHTER.

THE Relieving Officer of a large Poor-Law Union was conducting me over a Pauper Lunatic Asylum. There was the usual variety of cases; all interesting, all distressing. I cannot say that I was much gratified by the inspection; for, to tell the truth, I could not see myself surrounded by poor unfortunates, for whose wandering fancies no one could answer, without many half-shudders and whole misgivings. One of the keepers, of course, accompanied us. We suddenly came on a painful scene. Two athletic men—patients—had quarrelled, and fallen to blows. Three attendants were trying, ineffectually, to separate them.

"Wait one moment, gentlemen," said our guide, "I must lend a hand here," and he went to assist his comrades.

B

"Need we wait for him?" I asked the Relieving Officer. "I shall be rather glad to depart."

"Oh dear, no," was the reply; "I know the way out. Through this door, sir."

We passed into another room, in which were several women. One of them spoke to my companion.

"You would like to see my letter, Mr. Jones; it will tell you—"

"No, thank you, not now," answered the Relieving Officer, quickening his pace a little, and whispering in my ear, "Awkward customer—would make nothing of flooring us both: come along."

It was a long room we had to traverse, and we strode to the other end in a very few seconds. My companion had just opened the door, when, horror! a heavy tramp was heard; the Relieving Officer's rubicund face blanched; the lunatic was upon us. Upon *us?*—no; upon *him;* for, with shame I confess it, I rushed through the open door, leaving my unlucky conductor in a situation anything but pleasant. However, no harm befell him, for he followed me almost directly.

"I don't care to say more to that poor woman than I can help," he observed; "for though they tell me her life hangs on a thread (she's suffering from disease of the heart), her arm's anything but a feather. When the fit is on her, she's a perfect wonder. Be hanged, if she isn't coming after us!"

So she was. Reader, stalwart men as we were, we ran for it—down a passage, through another room, along

Recollections Of A Relieving Officer

RECOLLECTIONS

OF A

RELIEVING OFFICER

BY

FRANCIS W. ROWSELL, C.B., C.M.G.

LATE ENGLISH COMMISSIONER FOR THE DOMAINS IN EGYPT, FORMERLY
DIRECTOR OF CONTRACTS AT THE ADMIRALTY

LONDON
JOHN AND ROBERT MAXWELL
MILTON HOUSE, SHOE LANE, FLEET STREET
AND
85 ST. BRIDE STREET, E.C.

CONTENTS.

TALE   PAGE

    I. THE CHAIRMAN'S DAUGHTER .   .   .   1

   II. THE HAUNTED FIELD   .   .   .   14

  III. THE DEATH IN THE INFIRMARY   . .   31

   IV. THE REALLY DESERVING .   .   .   44

    V. SUSAN MARKHAM'S CHRISTMAS DINNER . 56

   VI. UPS AND DOWNS   66

  VII. THE ROBBERY OF THE OUT-RELIEF MONEY 79

VIII. BUBBLE FOR GUARDIAN .   .   .   90

   IX. THE STEP-MOTHER 104

    X. DESPERATE DEBORAH   .   .   . 123

   XI. RETRIBUTION 134

  XII. THE ELECTION OF A MEDICAL OFFICER . 148

 XIII. THE MIDNIGHT AFFRAY .   .   . 161

  XIV. MR. JONES IN A LITTLE DIFFICULTY . 174

  XV. THE BEDRIDDEN PAUPER   .   . 185

 XVI. THE INFIRMARY VISITOR   .   . 200

XVII. DIED THROUGH STARVATION .   . 210

XVIII. MR. FLACK'S MARRIAGE .   .   . 225

 XIX. A RELIEVING OFFICER'S DANGERS . . 239

a hall, and then we were in the Superintendent's apartments, and consequently free from pursuit.

While lunching with the Superintendent, we acquainted him with the mishap which had so nearly occurred to us.

"Poor Annette Worley!" said Mr. Spyers. "Her story is a sad one. Mr. Jones will tell it you. It is worth hearing."

PART I.

The following was the substance of the Relieving Officer's narrative :—

Mr. Hardman Selby was a great man in his own district in the West of England. He was very rich, very dictatorial, and very ill-tempered. He had been long a widower, with one child. Annette Selby was, ten years ago, a beautiful girl. She was doated on by her father, who provided for her every luxury she desired. Happy Annette Selby! Yet you have seen her to-day, a raving madwoman, in a Pauper Lunatic Asylum.

The sins of the fathers are visited upon the children. Hardman Selby was, in his wrath, awful to look upon, terrible to be near. In her fits of passion, Annette Selby was a very fiend.

Well, all around were well-nigh perfect slaves; so what matter? Tenants, dependants, servants, crouched and fawned, cursed, hated, and obeyed; so the father's wrath and the daughter's vehemence did no great harm, save to themselves, mentally and bodily.

Annette had just turned twenty, when, one day, her father intimated to her that Captain Wyerly would be their guest for a few weeks. The Captain came. He was an attractive, well-educated man of five-and-twenty. Of course he fell in love with Annette. Every man fell in love with her at first sight, and remained in love with her until she showed her colours, and then he immediately withdrew. But Captain Wyerly had to pass half-a-dozen weeks with Annette, whether he would or no. For Mr. Selby had arranged it; Captain Wyerly was not only to love Annette, but to marry her; and for Mr. Selby's will not to be carried out! Mercy!

Things took the proper course. The lady and gentleman acted with perfect propriety. Mr. Selby's resolution was implicitly fulfilled. Now, who was Captain Wyerly? Oh, of course, everything that was satisfactory. He was the only nephew of that fearfully-wealthy old bachelor, Sir John Larby, and Sir John had just had notice to go where none of his bullion could follow him.

" I am sorry to say, sir, that I must leave you, and that immediately," said Captain Wyerly, coming down to breakfast one morning with an open letter in his hand. " Sir John is at the point of death."

Of course expressions of sympathy were the response; but, to tell the truth, there was a smile of satisfaction on the faces of both father and daughter, as they uttered them.

"You will return to us as soon as you can?"

"Most certainly I will."

"You will have a great deal to attend to," remarked Mr. Selby. "In the case of such an enormous property as Sir John's, much labour will be required to arrange all things, and this labour must devolve—"

"Upon me," said the Captain. "There is no one else, you know."

"Not a single other relative, I believe." (Mr. Selby had devoted months to the satisfying himself on the point.)

"Not one; and, what is more, I believe he has never had the slightest affection for anything or anybody in this world, save myself and his bulldog."

"A kind, good soul," murmured Mr. Selby, without the least touch of irony in his tone. "Farewell, Captain, for a short time; and then return, to receive this roof as your abode."

This remark referred to the Captain's having been formally recognised by her father as Annette's future husband. And Annette herself—had she truly accepted him? With her whole heart—her strong, passionate heart—she loved him. His was a determined will, and he had conquered her's. She was, in the most absolute sense, his.

A fortnight passed. The scene was again the breakfast room; but this time it was Mr. Selby who appeared with the open letter. What was the matter with him? He gasped, and tried in vain to speak. Annette took the letter. It conveyed startling news. Sir John Larby was dead; and no sooner was he dead, than it came to light that many years ago he had been secretly married to his scullery maid, who now appeared as his widow, with four children. It was all revealed in the will, and the property, save a legacy to Captain Wyerly, was entirely left to the late Sally Mobbs, now Lady Larby.

For some minutes father and daughter gazed at each other without speaking.

"He never enters the house again," growled Mr. Selby. "An insolent impostor!"

It was not easy to see where the imposture lay, as regarded the Captain. So thought Annette, and in her heart she said, "The gold had no influence with me. Penniless though he be, I will not forsake him."

But not a word to her father. Discussions, she knew, would be worse than useless. There must be sacrifice without debate.

Then swiftly there passed communications which had these results:—a secret preparation, many tears, a meeting, a flight, a private marriage, and a roaring, as of a maddened lion, which almost shook the walls of Selby House.

After a time there came the usual appeal for forgiveness. It was unanswered. A year passed, and there came another very painful letter. The treacherous

husband had gone no one knew whither, and the
stricken wife and sorrowing daughter lay with her
sickly infant in a garret in London. To that letter
went this reply :

"You should have known me better than to apply
to me. I feed the birds at our parlour-window as we
used to do of old. I would not give you a loaf of bread
to save you from the workhouse. Each Saturday old
blind Billy still has from me the sixpence you used to
put into his hand when you were my daughter Annette.
I would not now give you, yourself, sixpence, to screen
you from a prison. Trouble me no more—begone !"

No more applications came after this, and Mr. Selby
went abroad for several years.

PART II.

IT was a drear November day, foggy and wretched.
Everybody within doors drew close to the fire-side, and
marvelled at the misery that had no fire-side to which
to draw. As the snow falls, and the keen blast causes
the house to rock, and the very incarnation of horror
seems abroad, seeking to clutch and press the breath
from out of all poor wayfarers whom he may meet with,
we, all of us, more or less, wonder what in the world
can save such as are lowly and poverty-stricken, from
utter desperation and raving madness.

A woman, apparently in the last stage of distress,
with an infant in her arms, staggered into a Relief
Office.

"Now, what is it you want?" inquired a surly functionary, from behind a counter, as though anybody finding their way in there for relief were an idea never for a moment occurring to his mind.

"I want bread; I starve," was the reply, in a hoarse voice.

"If you had bought a penny loaf instead of that last glass of gin," suggested the acute official, "it would have done you more good, and you needn't have come here."

"That isn't your business," replied the woman, "and so don't you meddle with it. I want bread."

"Then you won't have any."

"I'll break the windows."

"Do; and you'll go to prison."

"I tell you I'm starving. Give me a night's lodging."

The officer scanned the applicant.

"You casual paupers will ruin us. There—there's an order for the workhouse."

The miserable being received the order, and drawing round the unfortunate little creature on her bosom the tattered remnants of an old black shawl, staggered from the office to journey to the workhouse, which was some distance off.

Now how it came to pass none can tell, but the road to the workhouse was never taken, or, if taken, was soon widely departed from. Stumbling onwards through snow and mud, numbed and half-blinded, yet retaining

the power to advance, and exercising it with strange
determination, that forlorn woman, still lugging her
child to her bosom, travelled many, many miles; and it
was at the entrance of a village, a great distance from
town, that she first stopped and asked of a countryman
"the way to the House." It so happened that there
was a workhouse nigh at hand, and having been directed
accordingly, the wanderer, with almost a last effort,
reached the door, and dropped senseless. Thus she was
presently found, and carried indoors. She was then
searched, but nothing whatever was found upon her,
even the order for relief which had been given her having been lost in the long, sad journey. By degrees consciousness was partially restored, but memory seemed
to have entirely departed, and reason itself but flick-
ered.

What was to be done with such a case? The guardians
of that union, like the guardians of all other unions,
had a great dislike to more permanent burdens than
were absolutely necessary. Was there no possibility of
learning where the woman was chargeable, so that she
might be "passed to her parish?" The Relieving Officer
was desired to bring up the would-be drain on the
parish coffers before the board sitting in solemn con-
clave.

Now in this neighbourhood stood Selby House, and
to his mansion had lately returned Hardman Selby, Esq.,
after several years' absence on foreign travel. Little bene-
fited he looked by his wanderings. He was stout in body,

and full and flushed in face; but the village doctor shook his head, and remarked to a friend that the Squire had only come back from a long journey to take a longer, and one from which he would not return. However, the country round about manifested great delight at the reappearance of the wealthy invalid, and amongst other honours shown him, was the re-electing him Chairman of the Board of Guardians to the Poor.

It was, therefore, before Mr. Selby, as chairman, and a numerous assemblage of the Board, that Mr. Jones, the Relieving Officer, brought that poor, wretched woman. A great patch covered one eye and her left temple, which had been sorely bruised and cut when she fell at the Workhouse door. Her long black hair had only been partially cleansed, and so hung matted and dirty about her choulders. She was still in the deplorable attire in which she was found, and still she grasped her infant, for she would not part with it for an instant.

" Some mystery about the case," remarked the Relieving Officer, in a low tone; " I can make nothing of her; but whether she will not or cannot answer questions, I really do not know."

" Where do you come from, woman?" inquired Mr. Selby, authoritatively (in the old style, reader).

" Who asks me such a question as that?" was the counter-interrogation, and in a tone of pride which caused Mr. Selby to stare, but which only led the Relieving Officer to touch his forehead significantly.

" You are married," said one of the guardians, look-ing at a handsome wedding-ring on the woman's finger.

Not a word.

" Come, you must tell us something about yourself," said the Chairman, rather angrily. " Where's your husband ?"

There was one of the guardians, a good-natured old gentleman, by name Mr. Potts, who was made a butt by the guardians generally. Mr. Potts chanced to be seated close by where the woman was standing. On the Chairman putting the last question, the infant on the woman's arms suddenly leaped up, and struggled towards Mr. Potts.

" Dada ! my dada !" it shrieked in ecstasy.

" Halloa, Potts ! halloa !" cried a number of the guardians ; " what have you been about, Potts ?"

Mr. Potts grew crimson at this unexpected attack, and, in his confusion, leant forward affectionately to the child, and looked it attentively in the face.

" There can't be a question, Potts. It's the very image of you," cried a jocose Guardian.

" Now, if ye would all like to know who I am, and where I came from," suddenly exclaimed the woman, " why, now I've got it all written down in a letter which I'll show to that gentleman in the chair—to no one else, only to him. I seem to think I know him."

" She can have no letter," observed the Relieving Officer, " she has been searched."

" Hasn't she, though ?" retorted the woman, with all

that horrible look of cunning which often characterizes madness. And from underneath her masses of hair she drew forth a very solid piece of paper, which she handed mysteriously to the Chairman.

Mr. Selby examined it through his eyeglass.

"I cannot make out a word of it," he said. "Do you mind some one else reading it? It isn't a love-letter, is it?"

"Oh, no, it isn't a love-letter," said the woman. "Aye, he may read it," (seeing the letter handed to Mr. Potts).

"Here, Mr. Potts, you read aloud," said the Chairman; "but stay, don't do it if you find it lets us into any awkward secrets; we won't be hard upon you, Mr. Potts;" and Mr. Selby laughed more heartily than he had done for many a day, and the guardians joined.

Mr. Potts, half angry, and so confused that he hardly knew what he was doing, then read, in a loud tone, the following letter :—

"You should have known me better than to apply to me. I feed the birds at our parlour-window as we used to do of old. I would not give you a loaf of bread to save you from the workhouse. Each Saturday, old blind Billy still has from me the sixpence you used to put into his hands, when you were my daughter Annette. I would not now give you, yourself, sixpence to screen you from a prison. Trouble me no more—begone!"

Mr. Selby, who during the reading of the letter had

seemed bewildered, at its close sprung towards the wo-man, and holding her in both arms (she looking vacantly in his face the while) gazed at her intently. He then turned quietly, as though to walk back to his seat, when he encountered that foe who is always spying and dodging after every living being that walks the earth—death. He fell, and was gone.

The Board broke up in the utmost alarm and confu-sion. Slowly the light which had first entered hazily into the mind of Mr. Potts, shone upon the other members.

All Mr. Selby's property passed by his will to different charities. What was to be done with that poor out-cast? Her case was inquired into by a few friends of her girlhood; but guilt and misery came into view so strongly, that they shrunk back in horror. Ulti-mately an arrangement was made for her in a Pauper Lunatic Asylum, where she was received under a slightly altered name, and treated with special kindness and consideration.

"But she won't need anybody's kindness long," said Mr. Jones, in conclusion. "The same disease of the heart which killed her father, is killing her. She will be at rest soon."

II.—THE HAUNTED FIELD.

A stout, red-faced man, leaning over a churchyard wall, gazing pensively at a tomb-stone, is a sight rather calculated to induce a smile; and the tendency is not diminished, when we know the person to be a Relieving Officer under the New Poor Law.

But thus occupied I saw Mr. Jones, one wintry afternoon.

"Why, Mr. Jones," I cried, "how now? Selecting a choice spot for yourself, eh?"

"No, sir," he replied. "Where I shall rest my bones is a matter which never troubles me. I'm looking at poor old Nancy Wrekin's grave, in which she's been placed this afternoon."

"A pauper, was she?"

"Yes; she'd been one almost from the commencement of the union."

"Anything peculiar in her case? because, you know, I'm fond of hearing your little histories."

"Yes, there was something very peculiar."

"Then pray tell me all about it." And as we walked together to the town, Mr. Jones furnished me with the following narrative:—

We Relieving Officers always have been, and, I take it, always will be, thoroughly hated by the poor. The fact is, they accept our relief with the greatest repug-

nance, and they know we don't give more than we can
help, and what we do give we would rather withhold.
Now, while this applies to the regular or "settled"
poor, as they are termed, it is strongly the case with
the vagrant poor, who merely receive some slight assistance (some bread or a night's lodging), and pass on
their way. These applicants are, for the most part, a
wretchedly degraded set, and often occasion considerable
disturbance.

One November afternoon, several years ago, I was
sitting in my little inner room in the Union Office, and
my assistant (for this Union, as you know, covers a
large extent of ground, and I could not possibly get on
without help) was in the outer room distributing relief.
Suddenly, I heard loud talking; the next moment,
looking through the glass partition, I saw a huge lump
of bread come flying through the air, at my assistant's
head. Then arose a terrific storm. "Go along with
you, you hussy." "I won't go—give me the money,
you villain." "You shan't have a farthing, you drunken
old creature." "Then I'll break every pane of glass
in the place" (the usual mode of vengeance, by the
bye). "Will you? I'll have you marched off pretty
quick, my lady." Here I made my appearance, and
inquired the reason of the disturbance.

"I can't make out whether she's tipsy or cracked,"
replied Mr. Flack, referring to an old woman standing
at the open door, and grinding her teeth with rage.
"She says she don't want anything for herself, but she

must have five shillings for her mistress. Her mistress, forsooth! A pretty pass we are coming to. A mistress sends her servant to the Relief Office for five shillings!"

"Now, that's another lie of yours," screamed the old woman. "My mistress did nothing of the sort; but she wants the money, and you give it me, you monster, or I'll tear the place—I'll smash the windows—I'll kill you with stones," she yelled.

"You're a nice customer," said I. "Who is this mistress of yours?"

"I'm not going to tell you."

"Then you'll please to walk away."

"No, I won't. I'll please to break the windows," and a pane was demolished in a twinkling.

"Ah! that's too amusing to last," cried I, hastening round, and catching the old woman's arm.

"Halloa! are you going into a fit?" I inquired in alarm, for immediately the poor creature slipped from me on to the floor.

She did not reply, for she *was* in a fit, and commiserating her condition, though indignant at her wanton outrage, I had her carefully removed to the workhouse.

It was dark when I left the Union Office that evening, to walk to my home, which was about a mile out of the town. The last part of my way lay through a little piece of field, which had an evil character in the neighbourhood. The reason I could never exactly learn; but the story went, that in that field, once at least in every year, at night time, there appeared a female figure, clothed in white, and that from this apparition there issued sighs and moans most grievous to listen to.   I had traversed the field at night hundreds of times, and not a vestige of any female in white had I seen ; so I was, of course, an unbeliever in the tale. This evening, I had just stepped over the stile, when— I must confess, very much to my amazement—the sound of deep sobbing came distinctly to my ear.   I really do not see why I should not own, further, that my heart's action increased a trifle, as I peered about to see the cause ; and that when, a few yards off, I could perceive a white figure making towards me, I felt an unusual perspiration overspread my forehead.

It *was* a woman, all in white, too, and crying bitterly.

"Now, Mr. Jones, don't be such an arrant fool," said I to myself, as I half turned to retreat.   At the same moment, down fell the figure on the grass.   I went to it.   It was no spectre, but a poor woman, evidently very ill, and in great trouble.   I elicited from her that she had set out from her cottage, a little distance off, to seek her servant, who had left her some hours before to go into the town.   Questioning a little more closely, I discovered her to be the mistress of the infuriated old woman who had broken our window.   The truth appeared to be, that this distressed gentlewoman (for she was evidently above the common rank) was in a state of utter destitution, and that she and her faithful domestic were well nigh starving.   The cottage in which

C

they lived was completely secluded, and they had only been there a month, so that they were quite strangers in the neighbourhood. The servant had sallied forth to-day, unknown to her mistress, to obtain relief, having no notion, poor creature, of the inquiry and examination requisite before assistance could be given. I further learned that the sufferer had a husband, who, five weeks before, had sent her, with only a few pounds in her pocket, to this place, from London, intimating that he should join her in a month's time.

"Then you are now expecting him?" I said.

"Every day," was the reply; and as it was given, I staggered as though I had been wounded.

Wounded! Aye, I *was* wounded. The moon, shining forth suddenly, revealed to me a face not seen for years, but never forgotten—never forgotten—and never will be by me, this side of the grave.

Mary Leslie and I had both been born in a village ten miles distant. Suited for each other in every respect, I would have made her my wife, but she refused me. Her parents both died, and shortly after, she ran away from the guardianship of a very distant relative, with the son of a wealthy farmer. The farmer, who was furious, laid all the blame on Mary, and declared her an artful minx, who had inveigled his son. I know better. She was cruelly deceived, and Mark Sedley was a thorough villain.

And this poor face, so ghastly pale, so worn and wasted, was Mary's face.

'Mary!" I gasped.

Then she recognized me in a moment, and with a wild cry threw her arms about me. She told me all. The tale was dreadful, worse even than I expected, and I had been full of misgiving. Such neglect, such cruelty, such fiendish ingenuity in maliciousness, as had been exhibited towards the long-enduring and still loving wife, by her double-dyed scoundrel of a husband, I, with all my experience of life, could not have conceived. They had been in the depths of poverty; but either through pride, or an impression of its probable inutility, no application had been made to her husband's father for assistance. One day Selby had, as already stated, ordered her to depart from London for this town, giving no reason for the strange command, save that he was going a journey in which she could not accompany him, but that in a month's time he would be with her at any address which she should send to him, at a place he named. Here, then, Mary had arrived, and had found an abode in a cottage of two rooms, close at hand. Some scraps of furniture she had bought for a few shillings of the previous occupier. The woman she had with her was an old servant of her father's, whom she had met in London, and who would not leave her in her trouble.

"The scoundrel has deserted her," I thought. "Well, better so."

We reached the miserable dwelling, and Mary having entered, I hastened to the workhouse, where I found

old Nancy Wrekin frantic through being forcibly de-
tained, with the view of bringing her to account for
the broken window. I imparted to her my meeting
with her mistress, and the attendant circumstances, and
despatched her to Mrs. Sedley forthwith, sending with
her a porter laden with necessaries of various kinds.

I knew the elder Sedley was still living, so the next
morning I rode over to the village in which he resided,
and told him my painful discovery. He expressed
himself very pleased at the probability of seeing his son.

"A noble fellow, Mr. Jones," he said, with warmth;
"a manly, upright youth, as ever lived. Ah! what
might he not have been had he not been ruined by that
wretched, artful girl."

It made me mad to hear him speak thus; but it was
not wise to quarrel with him.

"However that may be, sir," I said, "she is your
son's wife, and I have told you her condition. Something must be done for her."

"Do you expect me to do anything for her, Mr.
Jones? Now, did you really come ten miles to ask me
to help her?"

"Certainly I did. Good heavens, Mr. Sedley, she
was starving—would have starved, had I not met her!
Come and see her."

"Yes, Mr. Jones, I will. When she's in her coffin,
you let me know, and I'll come—with pleasure."

Horrified and disgusted, I shrunk from the impla-
cable old brute, and returned home.

It was evening when I reached the Union Office. My assistant was affixing a placard to the notice-board outside.

"Here's a thing that has created a bit of a stir since you have been gone," he said; and he handed me a copy of the placard.

It announced a highway robbery, committed some fifteen miles off, described certain articles stolen, furnished close particulars of the robber, and offered a large reward for his apprehension.

"Not much chance of the rascal's escaping," remarked Mr. Flack. "Why, here's a complete portrait: —'Singularly prominent front upper teeth; scar on left cheek; very light hair; squints;' and a lot beside. Oh, he'll be nabbed, to a certainty."

I put the placard in my pocket, and proceeded to Mary Sedley's cottage. As I journeyed, the marked description of the as yet uncaptured robber dwelt on my mind. The reward was considerable—would be very welcome, even to me. Had I ever seen such?— Mercy! It flashed across my mind. Yes, there could be no mistake: the account tallied to a nicety with the exterior, as I knew it formerly, of Mark Sedley. I was exceedingly startled, and stopped to think, when my attention was suddenly arrested, as follows:—

I was in the "haunted field." On one side of me was a high bank, with a hedge at top. Above me, on the other side of this hedge were evidently two people talking. I listened; for the circumstance was strange in that place, and at that hour.

"You miserable magpie!" was growled in a manner which I knew well, though I had not heard it for years; "I've a good mind to pitch you over the hedge, you never-ending chatterer."

"Indeed, Mark!" I heard Mary Sedley reply, "I couldn't help it. I was dying—really dying for want of food."

"Dying! you've always been dying," grunted the scoundrel. "What now? Snivelling? What! at seeing me, is it? when the sight ought to make you happier than any queen. Now, take care! I only say, TAKE CARE!"

"There, I have done. Now, Mark, I've ceased crying; but don't be harsh; I'm very weak. Well, well, never mind. Now just tell me about these things. To whom did you say I was to take them?"

"To a man named Isaac Levy, in Hulk's Alley—just at the end of the town. You'll say you want to sell them, and he'll buy them. He'll ask no questions. To-morrow night, at ten o'clock, I'll come to you, and you'll have the money ready for me."

"But, Mark! now, Mark! I don't want to be curious; I won't ask you again where the articles came from; but do tell me where are you going to, and how long shall you be away this time; and, dear Mark, how am I to live?"

"How are you to live, eh? Look you, Mary, my

love, if you bother me with any more questions, you
shan't need to ask me again how you're to live. You
go and do what you're told; that's enough for you.
Now be off, double quick. And as for that old friend
of yours, Mr. Jones, I'll square accounts with him all
in good time. I'll cut his throat, Mary: you see if I
don't."

Then they seemed to separate. I watched about, and
saw Mary enter her cottage. I followed her immediately. She screamed loudly.

"Oh, Mr. Jones!" she gasped, sinking into a chair,
"how you frightened me."

"Mary Sedley," I said, somewhat sternly, taking up
a watch and other things which she had just laid on the
table, "where did these come from?"

"Oh, never mind! give them me. They are—"

"Mary, they are plunder; the fruits of a highway
robbery, and the robber was—"

"No, no, no!" she shrieked. "I will not believe it,"
she cried, divining my next speech.

"Now be calm, and let me tell you. I heard the
greater part of what passed between you and your husband just now. The man he named to you is a notorious receiver of stolen goods. And read this," and I
handed her the placard.

She read it.

"My God! this is worse than all," she wailed. "I
have starved and suffered well nigh unto death; yes,
almost to death, O, thank Heaven! but this is terrible."

"Now," I resumed, "there is but one course to be pursued. This ruffian has tortured you long enough. You must be released from him."

"How?"

"How? Why, through the law. He will be transported for life for this offence."

"But he is not in prison yet."

"No, but he soon will be. He is coming here to-morrow night, you know, and I shall have the officers ready for him."

"Ah, true," she said, staring vacantly at me. "I had forgotten. Yes, you would do that, of course."

She seemed bewildered, and, having learned from her that she expected the old servant to return immediately, I thought it best to leave her.

As I passed from the cottage, I pondered her strange look, and lingered at a short distance. The door opened gently. I saw her come forth, look about, close the door, and then run in the direction of the "haunted field" at the top of her speed. The idea immediately occurred to me, "She is seeking Sedley, to warn him against coming to-morrow night." I followed. It was perfectly dark, but her white dress enabled me to keep her in view. The field was reached. She wandered about, but found no one. She crossed again into the road, I still following as quietly as I could. Suddenly she stopped. She had come upon Sedley walking onwards. She touched him on the back, and he sprung round with a cry of alarm and an oath.

"It is I, Mark—I, Mary. I've had such a run, I can hardly speak; I want to tell—"

"You've followed me, have you? Curse you, body and soul. There," and he felled her to the earth.

"Mark, one word," said the victim, in a voice but little above a whisper. "It was to save—"

"What, you won't cease chattering? There, and there," and he kicked her as she lay. "Now go home."

Great God of Heaven! Through the mouth of that murdering villain was uttered the most merciful injunction which had fallen upon poor Mary Sedley's ear for many a long day, "Go home;" and she went home —to God.

Strong man as I am and was, I had turned sick at the first terrific blow, and before I could cry out, the second brutality had been committed. Then I shouted, and rushed forward. Sedley decamped, and I raised Mary, and ran with her, as quickly as I could, back to the cottage. The old servant was still absent. I laid the sufferer on her miserable couch, and leant over her.

She was dead. Terribly reduced and enfeebled as she had been, the violence had completed the tragedy. She was at peace. Her effort to save her husband had resulted in bringing liberty to herself. I threw open the little window, and as I gazed at the bright stars above me, I found myself again and again repeating—

"She is at peace. Thank God, she *is* gone home."

The old woman returned. I told her all that had taken place, and calmed her grief, which otherwise

would have been awkwardly uproarious, by promising
swift, sure vengeance on the murderer : at the thought
of which the devoted servant's eyes glistened, and she
promised secrecy and strict obedience to all my com-
mands.

The following night, our Inspector of Police, one of
his men, and I, set out from the town for the cottage.
It was wretched weather. The snow fell fast, the wind
blew, and the cold was piercing. We arrived. In the
course of the day Mary Sedley had been placed in her
humble coffin, and by its side sat Nancy Wrekin
watching; more faithful watcher never guarded the
dead.

It was arranged that the constable should lie crouched
under a hedge outside the cottage, while the Inspector
and I should remain in the bedroom, leaving only Nancy
in the sitting-room, so that Sedley might be fairly in
the house at the time of his capture, which would
thereby be rendered more easy. Thus we were all
placed, rather before nine o'clock, when the constable
outside came to tell us that a struggle seemed to be
going on a little distance off in the road ; but he could
only judge by sounds, for the night was so dark he could
see nothing at the smallest distance.

The man had scarcely returned to his hiding-place,
when the door of the cottage opened, and a most unexpected arrival took place. The elder Mr. Sedley
made his appearance. I met him as he entered. An
alarming spectacle he presented. He was so bedabbled

in snow and mud, with patches of blood, as scarcely to be recognizable.

"Good Heavens! Mr. Sedley," I exclaimed. "What you? And in that state!"

"And you, Mr. Jones? Why, what in the world brings you here? My story is soon told. I have been longer about a journey than I expected, and as it was such a night, and so late, I was making for your town, intending to sleep there. But you have queer folks about. Coming along the lane, where it was so dark I could not see my hand before me, there fell upon the back of my head an awful blow. I daresay the villain who gave it me spied, dark as it was, my plentiful crop of white hair, and that encouraged him to try to rob me. But he reckoned wrongly. I'm old, but I'm not weak, and with the aid of 'Finisher' here, I'll match any man now."

Here Mr. Sedley exhibited a formidable cudgel, from the knob of which, on the pressing a spring, there darted forth three or four little spikes.

"Well, I kept my legs, and in a moment my enemy and 'Finisher' had made acquaintance. The scoundrel gave an awful growl, and somehow managed to touch me in the chest, and nearly settled me. However, I rallied, and then, judging from his white coat, as well as I could, where his face would be, I brought 'Finisher' down upon him with my utmost strength. I believe it made an end of him. I hope it did. But I treated the villain to a third taste, and then I left him."

"Heaven pity the wretch! Why, you must have killed him!"

"Daresay—saved the hangman the trouble. But, old lady (to Nancy), if you could furnish me with—I feel a little shaken; but tell me, Mr. Jones, first, in whose place am I, that you should be here at this hour?"

Mauled as he had been, I was really sorry to excite him further; but I was so afraid of his vile son arriving, that I answered at once,—

"You are in your son Mark's cottage."

"Lord have mercy upon me! Then Mary Sedley lives here,—is in that other room, I suppose."

"She don't live here, but she lies in that other room."

"Eh?" he said, puzzled.

"Mr. Sedley," (and I could not help my voice trembling as I spoke), "come in with me and see her."

"No, no, no; I'll do nothing of the sort—I told you I wouldn't before. She'll plague me for assistance, and I'll give her none—not a penny."

"But you told me you would see her."

"*I* told you! you don't speak the truth, sir. In her coffin, I said, I would see her gladly, but never elsewhere—elsewhere never."

I threw open the door between the tiny rooms.

"Then see her in her coffin!" I cried; and taking advantage of his surprise, I moved him gently into the bedroom.

"My God!" he exclaimed, staggering from the coffin's side, "then she is really dead!"

"You have your wish. No doubt you feel your anticipated pleasure. She *is* dead."

"After all," said the old man, recovering himself, "it is better so. My son is free. You said he was coming here. Why, what is the policeman here for,— to watch the corpse?"

"Your son I expect almost immediately," I replied; "but I must tell you, there is no time to avoid it; he comes as a felon, and he will go away a prisoner,—read that placard."

He had great difficulty in doing it; but he saw enough to cause him to fall back against the wall, and groan in agony. Suddenly he sprang to the coffin.

"And this all through you!" he yelled, with demoniac fury, clenching his fist at the poor clay, and looking, besmeared as he was with blood, like a fiend incarnate. "You, you wretch—*you*, who seduced him; you, who took him from his home, from me; who ruined him; who—What was that?" he asked, in a whisper.

"For the love of God, Mary! open the door," said a faint voice without; "I am dying—some water—some water."

"It is *his* voice. I know it—I know it," gasped the old man, clutching me by the shoulder. "I have not forgotten it;" and before any of us, he had reached the door and opened it.

"Run away, Mark, run," he shouted. "They are waiting for you. Away for your life."

"He will never run again," said the inspector; and he dragged into the hut a prostrate body which lay outside.

Merciful heaven! what a sight it was! A man in a long white coat, saturated at the upper part with blood, and his forehead almost undistinguishable from bleeding wounds.

"Lord! Lord!" moaned the wretched being; "I am quite blind now—water—water—I'm dy—dy—" And he died.

Then the little hut, and the country round, rung with shouts of "Mark! Mark! Mark! My son! my son!" for reason left the miserable father; and escaping from our hold, he fled forth into the field, the darkness, the snow, the rain, reckless and mad.

He had slain his son, and in self-defence.

Mary was avenged.

III.—THE DEATH IN THE INFIRMARY.

"WHAT an astonishing congregation Mr. Bradley has!"
I remarked, one Sunday morning, to Mr. Jones, as
masses of people poured out of a Dissenting Chapel near
to us.

"Aye, and what a singularly effective preacher he is,"
was the reply. "I, being attached to the Church, do
not of course attend his ministry, but I have heard him
several times, and he was wonderfully eloquent and im-
pressive. You know his history?"

"No."

"Oh! I thought everybody knew it, for miles round."

"Indeed! Well, don't let me be different from everybody. Give it me as we go through the fields."

The always obliging Relieving Officer complied, and
the following was his story, with the addition of certain
particulars subsequently obtained by myself.

PART I.

There is no great town anywhere, but it embraces a
den of vice and crime. Where there is the most wealth,
there will be, a short way off, the worst poverty. In
the neighbourhood of the most magnificent abodes, telling of the highest refinement, will be found the most
squalid dwellings, evidencing utter wretchedness, sug-

gesting something worse. In the very heart of one of England's largest towns, several years before the New Poor Law came into operation, there was a long narrow street, named Blink Street. Around a house, even a shade or two dirtier and more repulsive-looking than its companions, there was gathered, one fine morning, a group of inhabitants of the ill-favoured locality.

"I saw his legs through the keyhole. I tell you, I'll swear it," cried the potboy from the tavern close by.

"I wish old Nick had been twenty-four hours sooner," exclaimed the landlord of the house, in a tone of great vexation. "Here's a bother," he continued, looking around for sympathy; "I lets a room for a week for a shilling, and the first thing a fellow does is—to go and hang hisself. Why, if he had told me what he wanted the room for, blow'd if I'd a let him have it for five— nor six neither—there's a plaguey mess now he's got me into. The beast ought to be ashamed of hisself, he ought."

A murmur of commiseration ran through the crowd.

"Well, well, Bill," cried a stout fellow, "suppose, instead of more palaver, we break open the door. Why, the poor devil may be alive, even now."

The crowd approving this suggestion, some half-dozen of its members rushed up the narrow staircase, and the two first men stopped in front of the door of the top back room.

"Now for it," said one, and in a moment the door was burst open.

The potboy had seen correctly. There were legs, and there was the rest of a body, and it was dead. For that old and final means, by which men in all ages have put an end to the ills of time, had been resorted to here. A man, whose countenance seemed to show that another day or two and disease would have saved him all trouble, and, at least, that *last* crime, had grown impatient, and with hot hand had thrown himself into the eternal world.

But there was something else in the room. On the floor was an infant, bleeding from a wound in the throat. It was not dead, for having, apparently, rolled itself underneath the corpse, its little hand was trying to clutch the dead man's feet, as though seeking aid.

Even the ruffians were shocked; not at the suicide—they looked indifferently at that—but at the poor child, and its forlorn condition.

"Here, I'll give it to my Sue," said one, and tenderly he carried it down stairs, and handed it to his wife without, who ran with it to a doctor's.

Presently the police arrived. In due time a coroner's inquest was held. Very little information was forthcoming. The only material testimony was that of the landlord, who stated that on the previous night to the discovery, a man and woman, with a child, presented themselves to him, and hired his room for a week, paying it in advance. That early the next morning the man had gone out, and shortly after, the woman followed. That the man then returned; of the woman

D

nothing more had been seen. That hearing nothing of the man for several hours, he had been induced to knock at the door of the room, and receiving no answer, the potboy, who happened to be on the stairs, had looked through the keyhole, and given an alarm.

No conclusion could be come to on this evidence, so an open verdict was returned. The suicide was buried, and the infant taken to the workhouse.

Workhouses never have been pleasant places, never will be; one may almost say, without uncharitableness, never should be. There is much more misery, my dear philanthropic friends, without the walls of a workhouse than within them. We know the extent of the privation endured by paupers "in the House;" there is a dead, drear blank, sad enough. Oh, we do not underrate it! but God only knows the suffering patiently borne by those whom a workhouse walls will never contain, because the outward moan, which would take them there, will never be uttered. It is not the man or woman who bends to the storm, and holds out the hand for the ungraciously proffered relief, who suffers so grievously. A brighter day comes to them. But there is no return of sunshine to those who are willing to suffer, willing to starve—to die; but let them die in peace, not in the workhouse—O God! not there!

The child was named after the man who had first taken him into his arms. I have not much to say about his boyhood. It was passed in the same way as the boyhood of nearly all the youngsters in the workhouse.

But he hated his domicile with a peculiar intensity, and when he had become a tolerably strong stripling he ran away. If I am to say the truth, I believe they made no hot search after him. A growing lad, eating his full allowance of food, and earning nothing, is an abomination to parish officers. The boy was well rid of, and the next poor-rate was a halfpenny in the pound less.

One afternoon, years afterwards, there presented herself at that workhouse door a woman in rags. It happened that all the officials were out; but there were waiting for one of them two youths, who were amusing themselves with a sparring match. The woman addressed one of the boys.

"Yes," replied the youngster. Then returning to his companion, he whispered, "I'll have some fun, Bob, you see. I'll turn relieving officer."

"There was—a—a poor infant, sir," gasped the woman, in most painful agitation, "who was brought here —several years ago. I—I—believe its—its father—des —destroyed himself."

"Yes; I remember it perfectly," said the youth, with a sedate countenance.

"I—I should have thought that—that you had been —hardly old enough to—to—" remarked the woman, with some surprise.

"Oh dear, yes; I remember all about it. Well, what do you—"

"Oh, sir, some one I know will be so—so glad to hear

any tidings of that—poor child. I saw fterwards in the newspaper that it was not killed."

"Bless you, no! it was alive, and kicked wonderfully, Didn't it, Bob?"

"More than any eel I ever saw," Bob acquiesced.

"But, alas! my poor woman."

"Oh, sir!"

"It *was* alive."

"But died?" shrieked the woman.

"Fell into the peas-soup, and was not found for days," replied the youth, mournfully.

A dreadful scream issued from the woman, and she sunk as in a fit.

"What a miserable donkey you are, Charley!" said the other youngster, "a most brutal donkey. Confound it! there'll be a row over this. My good woman, pray don't remain here. Here's five shillings for you—now let me lead you out," and he handed her out of the office. "Make haste away, as some one is coming who will take your money from you, for I've given it you against rules."

The woman looked up gratefully, and hurried off.

"If she hadn't been drunk, Bob," said Charley, as the former returned, "she'd have seen it was all fun."

"Never mind, Master Charley. What would you say if some one told you your child, if you had one—"

"There, drat it, don't preach."

"Had fallen into the peas-soup?"

"You be—what it would be—smothered."

PART II.

IN the infirmary of a workhouse, a great distance from that of which we have just been speaking, an old woman lay dying. The other occupants of the long, dull, sad room were much concerned in the event at hand. They looked and hoped for it most anxiously. And stay your reproaches, reader. You would have done the same had you been lying there sick and sorrowful yourself, for she was a dreadful old woman. Half-crazed as she was, one could hardly forgive her her loud blasphemous outcries and awful maledictions. She was on the brink of another world—what other world? And the answer seemed to come in a fresh burst of hideous curses, which almost deadened the air, so heavy were they with withering hate and horrid scorn.

"Now may heaven have mercy upon you, miserable Poll," squeaked an old crone of eighty, wheezing with asthma. "Recollect where you're a going, and say your prayers—"

"All in good time," shrieked Poll, with wonderful vigour. "I know where I'm going—where you'll soon follow, my love. There's room for us both."

"Be quiet, you hag!" roared a man at the other end of the room. "One would think that friend of yours had already got hold of you."

"Not a bit, my darling," was the ready reply. "He's busy with you at this moment. I see him. He's wri-

ting out your ticket for admission to his grand party.
You're to sit next to me," and a fiendish laugh accompanied the shocking joke.

For a few minutes there was a calm; then, starting
up in her bed, the old woman cried,—

"A parson! send for a parson. I want one."

The nurse went to the workhouse master. The chaplain had gone for the day—but with the master was a
dissenting minister, the Rev. Mr. Bradley, who offered
to attend the dying woman, and who, conducted by the
master, went to her bedside.

"Give me a short account of the case," he said to the
master, "that I may know how best to address and
deal with the sufferer."

"Poll Marley has been here some years," was the
reply. "She is not one of our regular poor. She was
brought in one day in a fit, and when she recovered, she
appeared to be in such a state of imbecility, that beyond
giving her name, she could furnish no account of herself whatever. We have taken care of her ever since.
It strikes me she is not so bad as she wishes us to think;
and that there are times when she could tell us much
more of herself than she chooses, I am convinced.
However, we have ceased questioning her. It won't
matter much, in a day or two, what parish she belongs
to; but I do wish she was better fitted for her last journey. Just hark at her now."

They had entered the infirmary, and a regular peal of
curses saluted them.

"Now you go!" yelled the miserable woman, starting up in her bed, and staring full at Mr. Bradley. "I'll have nothing to say to you. I've altered my mind—march!"

The minister quietly took her hand, and regarding her stedfastly, said,—"Listen to me for a few minutes, and then if you tell me to go, I'll go directly."

"Make short work of it," said the patient, sullenly. "You look a little better than the other fellow (meaning the chaplain); but you'll do me no good. For why? —for why? Ah! I'm a good mind—not now though —but by and .bye—at the last—the *very last*—not before."

What magic words could the minister have employed, in those few minutes, to have brought the terrible woman to that state of calmness in which the nurse beheld her, when she returned to the bedside? None, I fancy, reader, save the old words, which somehow or other have so often penetrated the apparently utterly hardened soul, and quickened it even in the final hour. Certain it is, that from that hour Poll Marley was wonderfully altered. She did not die for some days afterwards, and in the interval her intellect became clear and bright. By special permission, Mr. Bradley was constantly with her; and when the end came, her head rested on his arm. Thus she died.

There was perfect stillness in the room.

"Take courage — and hope," whispered the minister.

" I have no courage, and little hope," mourned the sufferer.

" Hush! why droop so ?   Sincere repentance——"

" Repentance," interrupted the dying woman.   " But ah! you don't know. Sir—sir!" she whispered, with a shuddering look round ; " is this the last—the *very last ?*"

" Death is at hand ; we cannot doubt it."

" Then I'll confess. Here. closer—closer. Years ago I committed two murders."

" Merciful Heaven !" exclaimed the minister, aghast. " But you must be wandering," he said, more calmly.

" I am quite sensible. New listen ! Long, long ago, I married William Marley, and we left our native village together. He used me most cruelly, most basely. I was mad and reckless. A baby was born. After wandering about for nearly a year, we entered a large town, and hired a room in the vilest neighbourhood I ever was in. I was well-nigh starving ; for though my husband ate, and drank, and had money, I was quite neglected. I have said I was mad. I am sure I was. My husband was ill. He said he could take care of me no longer, he must think of himself. He left the house where we were staying, and I never expected to see him again.

" What followed was his fault—not mine—so I have often thought and hoped. ' You shall not suffer longer,' I said to my baby boy ; and with a knife I thought 1 ended its days."

Mr. Bradley sprung from his seat, but instantly resumed it.

"Then I fled from the house, and went many miles away. A few days after, I read in a newspaper the suicide of my husband, who appeared to have returned to the room almost as soon as I had left it, and hung himself. I am his murderer. The sight of his child, dying, as he thought, no doubt, and by violence at my hand, as he must have concluded, probably turned his brain, and I am responsible for the result. But I have more to say. I killed my child too, though not at the time and in the manner I thought.

"Years rolled by—such years of wretchedness and crime! I could not forget my child. I had also read in the newspapers that it was expected he would recover, and he had been taken to the workhouse. I long resisted the prompting to go and make inquiry concerning him. I feared I might be recognized, or my questions would excite suspicion, and I might be brought to justice for the intended murder. At length I determined to run the risk, and journeyed many weary miles to the workhouse which had received my baby.

"I went to the door several times, and retreated. Ultimately, having drunk more than one glass of raw spirits at an inn close by, I entered the building, and asked about the child. He was dead, they told me. How or when he died, I think they told me too; but I considered myself his murderer likewise, and my poor brain only held the chief intelligence. I ran from the place, and—"

"It wasn't true, it wasn't true!" exclaimed Mr. Bradley, taking the hand of the dying woman.

"Sir!" she said, regarding him with faint wonder, for life was fleeting fast.

"Look at me, look at me," eagerly whispered the minister, turning back his hair with both his hands. "Can you form any idea what I should have been like when I was young? But it will be too late. Mother, I say, mother!" And he knelt beseechingly at the bedside.

Here there entered the room, and approached the bed (which had been removed into a corner, as far as possible from the other beds), one of the nurses.

"The hour for your medicine," she said, somewhat roughly; "sit up now, and take it, there's a good creature."

In a moment Mr. Bradley had thrust her away fiercely.

"Go along!" he cried. "Away with you!"

"Lawks, sir!" ejaculated the nurse, surprised and offended. "It's the doctor's orders, and she must have her physic." And she re-approached.

Mr. Bradley seized her by the throat, his eyes gleaming with fury.

"I'll kill you; I'll strangle you; I'll kill you instantly," he whispered. And the glare of madness was in his eyes.

"Lord ha' mercy on me! the minister's lost his senses," gasped the nurse, in great dismay.

Mr. Bradley flung her from him, and she ran with the alarming story to the master.

So gently that newly-found son raised toward him his dying mother.

"O God! but two minutes of life," he exclaimed; "only time for recognition. Mother, mother, I am your boy—preserved through many trials to many blessings! Say you know me—one word, just one word!" And he placed his ear to her lips.

"My boy!"

And another soul was gathered into the great store-house.

IV.—THE REALLY DESERVING.

" You must be able to discern between real and assumed distress in a moment, Mr. Jones."

" It is, certainly, very seldom that I get cheated," replied the Relieving Officer; " although some of them try uncommonly hard, and uncommonly well, too. Perhaps there comes in a poor, wretched object, in rags, and he stands shivering and whining in fashion to melt a heart of stone. Bless you, sir, if you were there, you'd ask no questions. You'd call out, ' Light a fire; get me blankets, warm the water for a bath; bring meat and bread and beer,' and you'd have the poor mortal surrounded with comforts and luxuries in five minutes— whereas I—what do I do? I look at him. Half a glance is enough. I let him groan a bit, and then, at the top of my voice, I say,

" ' Now, I tell you what it is, my fine fellow, just you walk out of this place, or I'll have you up before the magistrates in no time.'

" Now, am I not a brute?"

" Silence signifies assent, Mr. Jones."

" Well, but now, wait a bit. When I have addressed my ill-used, starving, coaxing, cringing, and crying friend, in this shockingly savage style, what does he say? Why, he drops the beseeching looks and the pitiful tone in a second, and sets to and abuses one like a demon."

"Well, I'm sorry, but upon my word I cannot be surprised."

"No; I daresay not; but, perhaps, you'd say it's my fault. Why, my dear sir, the probability is, that I have detected in that fellow a lazy, skulking vagabond, who roams about from place to place, never thinking of such a thing as honest work, but not ashamed to beg food and lodging at all the unions in the country. Have I a heart? Yes; I have a heart. I feel for the poor ratepayers in the by-streets of this large town, grinding, slaving, screwing to pay the poor-rates; I think of the privations, the misery, the, the—dull, heavy care—the, the—"

Mr. Jones was positively getting into a passion.

"My good friend," I expostulated, "don't be angry. We all know that Relieving Officers are the kindest, most benevolent of men, and—there, there; I won't say more about it."

He calmed instantly. "You were talking of my discernment," he said; "I *do* pride myself upon it, but I had a terrible knock-down blow once, a regular floorer."

"Good morning, sir." (The salutation to a stout, very pleasant-looking man who passed us.)

"Our chairman, Mr. Eardley, one of the best of men, sir."

"I quite agree. But what was that terrific affair you have just alluded to ?"

"Why, it was a practical joke played off upon me, through my boasting of my penetration, much as I have been doing now. Only on that occasion I was a great deal more vain. I've never quite recovered my discomfiture at being made a most melancholy dupe."

"Let's hear the story, if the narrative be not too painful."

"Oh dear, no; I'd suffer a hundred jokes at the same hands, the hands of two of the most amiable young men in the country. I mean the sons of our chairman, who has just passed us."

"They were lads at the time; a few years make all the difference at that period of life. You've heard me speak of Master Charley and Master Bob, before. As youngsters they were brimful of fun, carried to recklessness sometimes, and bringing results which they were sorry for. They had no fear of reproval from their father. In truth, I believe he helped them in their more artfully planned pieces of frolic, and I have no doubt he did in the one I am going to tell you of."

We stood together one day, chatting. Neither the boys nor their father ever had a morsel of pride. I could talk as freely to them as to my most intimate friends.

Master Bob said to me, "You're a clever fellow, Mr. Jones, to pick out the good and bad as you do. One would think they had different marks on them."

"So they have, Master Bob," I replied. "The really deserving show signs very different to the rascally impostors. Why, with the experience I've had, give me but one eye, and hold a bit of gauze before that, and I should still be able to tell an honest pauper from a cheat."

(What an idiot I was to talk in this bombastic style before such boys as those! I might have guessed what would come of it. A scheme would be devised to lay my conceit in the dust in no time.)

"Humph!" uttered Master Charley, musingly. "Yes, Mr. Jones, your power in that way is wonderful. I've seen it exercised often myself. A batch of paupers stands before you. You say to one—You're a really deserving fellow; and it turns out he *is* a really deserving fellow. You say to another, I know you are a cheat; and sure enough, he proves to be a cheat. Wonderful, Bob, isn't it?"

"Staggers me altogether," answered Bob; "he looks into 'em, and reads 'em like a book."

I was highly gratified. I patted Master Bob on the back, saying, "Yes, Master Bob, if ever you hear of any paupers getting over me, I'll give you and Master Charley a sovereign each,—there now!"

"A sovereign!" cried Charley; "well, that's liberal —it's worth trying for. Shall we see if we can 'do' Mr. Jones, Bob?"

"*Do Mr. Jones!*" exclaimed Bob, with affected amazement. "Bless you, Charley, what are you thinking of? But yet I don't mind trying. Mr. Jones, we'll see if we can't get that sovereign out of you."

"Oh! very good," I said. "By all means. You show me that I don't know the difference between the really deserving poor person and the fictitious tale-teller, and you shall quickly have the sovereign. But be on your guard, you know, in your fun. You may get some rubs, if you try any practical jokes—"

"We'll bear 'em—we'll bear 'em," they cried together: "we're not afraid of a tumble or so. Life and limbs safe—that's sufficient for us."

I knew that!—daring young scapegraces!

I guessed, of course, what they would be doing. They were both admirable mimics. Scores of times I have attended the private theatricals at their father's, and been astonished at their acting. They would have succeeded vastly on the stage, had no other profession been open to them. "Yes, they will dress up as paupers," I thought; "I shall have them coming to the office, and asking relief; and when they have got it, they will turn round and laugh at me, and I shall never hear the last of it. Ah! but they can't play the character of a pauper half well enough to trick me, clever as they are. I'll give them a dose if they try, and we'll see where the laugh will be." What a wretched end came of my vain boasting!

A day or two afterward, I was busy in the Union Office, attending to the case of two "casual" paupers, a poor woman (a widow) and her son, when in came two sturdy-looking tramps, and howled out a claim for relief. I surveyed them quietly. "Yes," I said to myself, "it's capital, it's first rate—not even your father, I think, would recognise you, my young friends. These rags, those brown faces, those abundant masses of false hair, those twisted features, those begrimed, coarse hands, and, beyond all, those marvellous tones— upon my word, it's all better even than I expected. But yet—but yet—Oh, dear Master Bob, and dear Master Charley—it's useless with me. I see through you in an instant."

I let them screech away for some minutes a long story about being two brothers, who had tramped all the way from Newcastle in search of work, and had now completely broken down.

"If you would but give us a loaf of bread and a shilling to help us on our road, we would ever bless you, kind master," whined the young scamp, Master Charley.

"Two poor twins, well nigh a starvin'," moaned his artful confederate. "Think, master, what would be mother's feelings if she could see them now."

I could hardly keep my countenance, but I did manage it.

"Hold your tongues, you young vagabonds," I shouted; " wait your turn—don't you see I'm engaged?"

They poked their fingers in the corners of their eyes, and retired against the wall, continuing to moan.

The case I had in hand, when they came in, had interested me not a little, for two reasons. In the first place, the applicants had travelled from a locality very

dear to me, many, many miles away, where resided near
relatives and loving friends of mine.   In the next place,
the case, though not uncommon, was a very sad one.
The poor widow had tried to carry on her late husband's
business, and had failed ; and now, with her only son,
she was endeavouring to make her way to a manufactur-
ing town a hundred miles off, where she had a dim
notion of finding friends.   But the idea of setting out
on such a journey, and in winter too, with only a few
shillings to start with, and borne only by limbs enfeebled by sickness and privations.   Of course, both
mother and son drooped and sank, and now were obliged
to come to a Workhouse to beg relief.

I was greatly touched, and was pained as to my course
with them.   My duty was to pass them to their parish,
which they had quitted ; but their real want was to be
helped on their journey.

"I am truly grieved," I said to the widow ; "but I
can do nothing for you, but send you back again ; and
really, I think that if you were under the protection of
your own parochial authorities," (fine words, truly,
reader, to cover the meaning 'if you went into your
own workhouse') "you would be better off than in
pursuing your very doubtful enterprise."

"I'll never go into a workhouse !" exclaimed the
widow, weeping passionately.   "I and my boy will
starve rather."

"Don't cry, mother—don't—don't," wailed the boy,
the tears pouring down his own cheeks.

"Ah, sir! when they who have been respectably brought up are told that there is nothing for them but the workhouse, you don't know how it cuts them to the very heart." And here the agonized woman folded her son in an earnest embrace, and they wept together. Suddenly the boy shrieked, "Oh, oh! she's dying!" And his mother fell backwards.

I had a miserable cold that day ; hid in the fender was a tumbler of mulled port wine. This I hastily handed to the boy, and bade him give it to his mother, which he did, and she revived. While she was taking it, Mr. Potts, the guardian, came in,—the very man I wanted.

"Pass them to their parish? Oh, dear, no," said Mr. Potts, when I had communicated the case to him. "Downright cruelty! Here, bother the parish funds! give them that." And he placed a sovereign in my hand.

It is in my recollection now, the ecstatic delight manifested by the poor couple when I gave them the present, hoping that it would help them effectually on their road. A shower of blessings came upon Mr. Potts and me, and moisture was perceptible about the kind-hearted guardian's eyes. I was considerably moved myself, and, to give a turn to the scene, I looked at my beautiful young gentlemen, who were lolling against the wall, and roared out,—

"You precious scamps! it is such as you who take the bread out of the mouths of truly deserving poor people like these."

"The gentleman is right," said the widow. "Why don't you work, young men?"

"Blow'd! We got no work to do, missus."

"You're lazy—you won't work!" cried the widow's son, supporting his mother's attack.

"You're wicked fellows!" screamed the widow. "I hope they'll send you to prison! I trust they'll beat you!"

I began to think the mulled wine had been rather too much for her.

"Not a morsel of bread do they get from me," said I, "until they've had an hour's stone-breaking. What is it, my good woman (seeing the widow advance again to speak to me)?"

"You said, sir, you had relatives and friends at D——. Oh, sir! would you—might I ask for just a scratch from your pen to one of them?—it might get us something to do, if our friends won't help us."

I saw no objection, so I wrote a few lines to a near relative at D——, and gave the note to the woman.

"There," I said, "now, I think, if you take this nice woollen shawl (and I handed her one from a store), you will have all I can manage for you. Good-day—wish you well on your journey."

And, with a fresh outburst of blessings, they departed.

"Now, young gentlemen," said I, "are you going to take your order for the stone-yard? Because, if not, you'll please to march."

To my great surprise, they said they would; so I

handed them a ticket for bread and meat, to be received
after they had done one hour's work in the stone-yard,
and they left the office.

"Well, if you're going to continue the joke with
spirit," said I to myself, "I'll match you;" and I directly sent a note to the master of the workhouse, telling
him to treat the lads with the utmost rigour, for I was
sure they were impostors, and ought to be made an
example of.

Just as I had concluded the note, I received a summons to attend a case at some distance, and I was absent
several hours. On my return, I went immediately into
the workhouse; I was met by one of the porters.

"O! sir, I'm so glad you're come; the master's out,
and Joe Tomkins is murdered, and he's just having some
beef tea, and both of 'em have had their heads shaved."

Selecting the chief feature in this not very lucid communication, I demanded the exact condition of Tomkins
(a "pauper assistant"), and the names of his assailants.

"Why, sir, you remember them ere boys you sent in
this morning, with a note. Well, we did give 'em an
uncommon stiff bit of work, sure-ly, and they growled
horrible. At last, one of 'em—he picks up a huge stone,
and he says, says he, to Tomkins, who was superin-
tendin' the work, and drinkin' his soup (for to-day's
soup-day—a wicked sinner he was as invented soup-
days in workuses!), 'There's somethin' more substantial
for yer, old chap.' And he threw the stone at him with
all his might, and knocked him to shivers."

"Good gracious!" I exclaimed, in equal alarm and astonishment. "What then?"

"Well, sir, we picked up his bits—."

"His bits! What, bits of his body?"

"No, sir, not his body; his basin, what I told you was broke, and he's had some beef tea instead."

"Well, well! But the lads—?"

"Yes, sir; well, they were in the 'Refractory Ward' in no time."

"Dear, dear, dear!" I muttered to myself, "what folly in them to carry their stupid joke so far! And they're there now, I suppose?"

"No, sir; they made such a row, that the Doctor thought they were drilirous, and they've been put in the Infirmary, and had their heads shaved."

I stayed for no more, but half "drilirous" myself, I rushed to the Infirmary.

"Show me the lads just admitted!" I cried.

"Yes, sir," replied the nurse; "there they are," pointing to two beds in the corner; "but, be careful, sir; they're—you know" (touching her forehead).

I ran to the unfortunates, and then I fell back. Then I went to them again, and stared at them. Lastly, I sat down on a chair, and the various beds performed a waltz, and the room was lit up with streaks of green flame.

The boys were no more Charley and Bob Eardley than the two porters. The poor wretched objects in the bed had not the least resemblance to them.

While I sat stupefied, a message came to me that Mr. Eardley, the chairman, wished to speak to me below. I ran down stairs. Mr. Eardley held out his hand, saying :—

"I've just looked in, Mr. Jones, to say I've heard my boys have been playing you a trick, and you have sent them into the stone-yard. Serve them right; quite right. There, you needn't say anything. *I know all about it.* Good-bye! good-bye!" and he quitted hastily.

"Good gracious!" muttered I to myself. "Is it after all, then, the case? Can they—" and I ran again to the Infirmary, and once more peered into the faces of the poor wretched lads, to make quite sure that they were not Masters Bob and Charley.

I had just satisfied myself completely on this point, and was pondering, in utter amazement, the meaning of the communication made to me by Mr. Eardley, when the porter brought me a parcel and a note. The latter was in Bob Eardley's handwriting, and was as follows :—

"Dear Mr. Jones,—With many blessings on your benevolent head, we return you a shawl, one sovereign, and a certain note of recommendation with which you recently favoured us to your relative at D——. *They have all served our purpose,* and now you had better bestow them upon some unfortunates, even *more* deserving than the

"*Really* deserving afflicted and destitute } Widow and Son,

"BOB and CHARLEY EARDLEY."

I gave the sovereign to the poor lad as a compensation
for my harshness, but the affair very materially diminished my stock of conceit, I can assure you, sir.
I never *shall* hear the last of it.   All the guardians
got hold of it; the whole Union got hold of it; the
paupers got hold of it; and, even now, I never recommend
to the Board any case as "really deserving," without
such a chorus of laughter arising, that I feel inclined to
knock my brains out with the chairman's hammer.

V.—SUSAN MARKHAM'S CHRISTMAS DINNER.

WE stood and saw them dining.   A painful sight it
was, that hundred and odd paupers feasting on Christmas-day.   Aye! I contend it was, reader, to the mind
that dived beneath the surface, and took in the long
past, the stern present, and the dark future at a glance.
Who amongst this sadly merry gathering dreamed, years
ago, that a Christmas-day would come when the old
fare would be eaten beneath a workhouse roof?   Be
happy, indeed! be comfortable! eat and drink!   Yes,
by all means serve out the carefully-weighed allow-
ances, and *command* enjoyment.   Gladden benevolent
hearts by recording in next day's newspaper how light
and life were sought to be introduced into the pauper's
dwelling for this day.   I do not say you are wrong,
quite the contrary; but do not think, do not pretend,

that the sorrows of pauperism fled at the sight of tenderly-carved roast beef and plum-pudding. Perhaps they did move a trifle at the unusual display. But it was *such* a trifle, and they so soon returned; driven back by thoughts of the old home—*gone by;* the self-respect—*gone by;* the many friends — *gone by;* the hopes, the fancies, expectations—*gone by;* the dark misfortunes, the dreary ruin *come,* and standing there rigid, and black, and unpitying.

"They *seem* to be enjoying themselves," I said to my companion, the Relieving Officer.

"Oh! and I daresay they are, to some extent, and after a fashion," was the not very buoyant reply. "For my part, if I were to come to the workhouse, and they were to offer me roast beef and plum-pudding on a Christmas-day, I think I should murder them."

Mr. Jones's thoughts were evidently running in the same direction as my own.

"What more can be done for them?" I asked.

"As things are—nothing," he replied. "Very few ought really to be here. Some should rather be in a jail; to others the hand of true charity should have preserved their own homes. Such as these will have no pleasure in their dinners to-day. But while I attend to some little matters for a moment, would you like to walk along the tables? You will see, at all events, that there is no stint of meat and drink."

I followed the suggestion, and strolled away from my companion to the other end of the room. The sight brought me but small gratification, and I was turning back, when my attention was attracted by an old woman sitting in a corner alone, with her dinner on a slab before her

"Do taste the plum-pudding," she said, earnestly—"it is so nice;" and she proffered a morsel on her fork.

I have a great horror of doubtful edibles and, though I complied, I did so with an ill grace.

"Beautiful!" I said, inwardly writhing.

"Didn't it go down you warm?" inquired the old dame, peering oddly into my face. "You thought it was the brandy; now, didn't you?" she cackled.

"Wonderfully strong spirit," said I, smiling.

"But it wasn't spirit. O, no!" returned the old woman. "Who's your undertaker?"

"Eh?" I exclaimed, aghast.

"Spirit! O, no, no! It was POISON! I put it in —all myself—all myself. Arsenic! lovely arsenic! He! he! he! he!" and the miserable creature laughed feebly, but with horrid delight.

I put my two hands on the spot whither the pudding had descended, and, for the moment, my head reeled; but I recovered myself directly, and returned to Mr. Jones, to whom I narrated the conversation.

"Ah, yes," he said, "there's no harm done. It's poor Susan Markham. Her senses have left her; but she's quite harmless, and we let her come in to dinner. Poor, wretched old woman, this day five years her crazed wits did indeed make a house of mourning."

"If we don't do something to get rid of these rats, we shall have the house down about our ears, John, that's very certain."

Thus spoke Mrs. Markham to her husband as they sat at breakfast one morning.

John Markham was not a very important person in the world's eyes. He was only a labourer on Squire Bush's estate, but he had constant work, was strong and healthy, and had a good wife, and somehow managed to be tolerably cheerful.

"Well—that won't do, Mary, at the very time when we want to make it bigger, will it?" asked John, in allusion to an expected event which would render more instead of less house-room necessary. "We must get some poison for them. When I go to-night to fetch mother, I'll buy some arsenic, and the rats shall have a feed this Christmas-eve."

"I say, John, you know I'm as fond of your mother as you can be, so there needs no excuse for what I'm going to say—but is she quite recovered? because you know that I am so mortal frightened of mad people, that really I—"

"She isn't mad," interrupted John, testily.

"Well, you know she has been very queer."

"True, Polly, but she's old—very old — and weak rather, both in mind and body. Poll, if we live to that age, they'll call us mad. When I saw the doctor last week, he told me that mother was just well again; and there's Nancy Jones, who's got the care of her, will tell you that, except she's always at some mischief or other, mother's as harmless as you or I. Then I say mother shall have her Christmas dinner under this roof, or my name's not John Markham."

It might have been a spirited line of conduct on the part of Mrs. Markham, if, in reply, she had burst out in this fashion—"Then, I say, John Markham, as sure as my name's Mary Markham, if you bring your mother here, mad as she is, I'll—&c., &c." But when John was pettish Mary would be silent, so there was very little jangling in that cottage. Mary did not by any means relish the idea of Mrs. Markham's (senior) company, but her husband wished it, and that was enough.

In the evening, the poor old woman was fetched by her son from the neighbouring village, where she had been some time under care of a nurse.

"Here's mother," cried John, heartily, to his wife; "and as strong and well as ever you were, ain't you, mother?"

"Oh! aye, I'se very well," replied his mother. "How's the mad dog, John?"

"The mad dog, mother?"

"Ah! sure enough—the mad dog, John. She's here—I know her—keep her off me, John! she'll bite me," cried the afflicted old lady, pointing at her son's wife, and shrinking from her in great alarm.

"Bless me, mother!" exclaimed John, in consternation at this dubious evidence of his parent's recovery, "that's Poll—no mad dogs here, nor anything else

mad," he added, cheerfully; "come, shake hands with
Poll!"

It would be hard to say which Mrs. Markham shrunk
most from this manifestation of good will; but it was
accomplished—the ancient dame muttering the while
something about "puppies."

"There — that's right," cried John.   "And now,
Poll, there's something for your friends," and he threw
a very small packet on the table.

"This is the poison, is it, John?"

"Yes, and be very careful how you use it—but I
need not tell you that."

"My dear," said the elder Mrs. Markham, sidling
again to Mary, "let me have that."

"Mercy! no, not on any account!" cried her son,
interposing.

"I say yes," replied the old lady, imperiously.   "I
know best how to use it; I'll give it her in a piece of
meat; you remember how well I managed with your
father's dog when it went mad, and I poisoned him?"

The reply to this appalling suggestion was a burst of
tears from the intended victim, and an exclamation of
horror from her startled husband.

"Mercy on me!" he groaned.   "Why, you was right
as a trivet, mother, when we started.   What *can* have
brought it on again?"

To this inquiry the old lady merely vouchsafed a look
of contempt, mumbling something about the nonsense
of such a fuss about the loss of a mad dog; "and a

very shabby looking one, too," she added, glancing
scornfully at poor Mrs. Markham, junior.

So soon as he could get an opportunity, John withdrew his wife into another room, and took council with
her as to what was to be done.

"Poor mother!" he said, mournfully. "I am so
disappointed; but I must take her back again directly;
that is quite clear."

To this, his wife, good-hearted woman as she was,
decidedly objected, urging that the poor old woman
might shake off the strange notion that somehow had
possessed her, and that, at all events, they would see
the effect of a night's rest. She might be all right in
the morning.

This they agreed to, and Mrs. Markham said she
would keep her bedroom for the rest of the evening, so
that the sight of her might not continue the irritation
which they wanted to allay.

The next morning Mrs. Markham, senior, certainly
seemed the most lively of the party. She had slept
soundly, and was brisk and strong. John and his wife
had scarcely closed their eyes. Mrs. Markham had done
nothing but cry out,—"Here she comes, John;" and
had fancied a hundred times that the poor mad woman,
who lay sleeping quietly in the next room, was standing
over her with a carving knife. Morning dawned at
length, and the party assembled at breakfast.

The rest seemed to have worked wonders. No more
allusion to the mad dog—no more shrinking and shud-

dering. The patient seemed to have changed once more to a lively, good-tempered, chatty old dame,—a very pleasant companion. John and his wife were delighted.

I apprehend there is no perfect explanation of the subtle minutiæ of insanity, its ebbings and flowings, its secret workings and influences. Mrs. Markham, senior, was, in reality, worse that morning than she had been the night before. The previous night she, at least, showed that she was mad. In the morning she was more mad, because she concealed her madness, hugged it within her, and kept it more closely to her. Oh, those cases are dreadful! I don't much mind hearing a man rave in delirium tremens. The inflammation in his brain will, probably, have subsided in a day or two, and there will be nothing the matter with him. But I have a great horror of madness in cases where it is not merely wildness or incoherency, but where it assumes a defined shape,—is, in fact, a consistent inconsistency, and comes and goes when and how we know not. Poor old Mrs. Markham's case was one in point.

How busy she was that day, and so glad to be of service! Her eyes glistened at being employed in household work. It was Christmas-day. The little cottage had to be made very clean and tidy, and the labour fell principally, at her own request, on John's mother, for his wife, just then, could do but little. And then there was the pudding. John remembered his mother's famous pudding in the old time, and rejoiced that once again he should eat a Christmas pudding made by his old mother's hands. Once again, John,—but only once!

The first part of the dinner was disposed of, and the said pudding made its appearance. It was a noble affair, a great deal too large for such a party; but it was a fault on the right side, and John merely laughed.

"I was determined you should have enough of it," cried the old lady, rubbing her hands. "Now eat away, eat away!"

And all three began vigorously.

Such a scamper of rats! overhead, underneath, round about!

"Mercy on us," exclaimed John, "did anybody ever hear the like of that? We shall be eaten alive."

"Give 'em a bit of the pudding," said Mrs. Markham, senior.

"No; that I certainly won't," replied John. "Why, Mary, how is it you—"

"Bless me!" interrupted his wife, "I quite forgot. You mean the poison, John. I forgot all about it."

"Why, you took it away with you last night."

"No, I did not."

"You didn't! What became of it then?"

Then there came from that miserable old woman such a scream of wild delight, as she rose from her chair, and clapped her hands again and again in the exuberance of her mad ecstacy.

"Wasn't it good?" she cried; "didn't you feel it! didn't it go down you *warm?*" she shrieked.

John and his wife jumped to their feet, aghast and shivering.

"Lord love you, mother, what went down?" asked John, catching the old lady by the arm.

"The pudding—the pudding," she shouted; "I knew how to make it hot and nice and comfortable. You thought it was brandy—but it was something better than that—it was arsenic—lovely arsenic—I knew how, I knew."

John heard no more. He rushed from the house almost as mad as his poor relative. Most fortunately he met, within a yard or two, the man of all others he wished to see—the village doctor. The story was told in a moment, and a variety of remedies were directly in operation.

Now what could have caused that unfortunate old dame to have spoken as she did? There was no arsenic in the pudding. The paper containing the poison was found afterwards on the mantelpiece, and the quantity was ascertained to be precisely the same as that John had purchased. So there was no mischief done. Alas! yes, there was,—almost as much as though the lunatic had spoken the truth. Mary Markham, as has been intimated, was close upon her confinement. The terrible shock prostrated and, in effect, killed her. The delivery of a dead child, a high fever, raving madness, and a painful death, were the dark events crowded into a few days. And there was no light in that dwelling afterwards for poor John. Another year saw another coffin passing that threshold, and Mary Markham's humble grave was opened to receive another occupant.

VI.—UPS AND DOWNS.

"It is a strange story, Mr. Jones."

"Yes, sir," was the reply of the New Poor Law functionary, "it is another illustration of the 'ups and downs' of this life."

PART I.

"Now, then, where are you shoving to?"

This interrogatory, more forcible than elegant, is not often heard in a country town; but it did issue one night from a poorly-dressed person, who was hastening along the main street of Bramblestone, and against whom, at a sharp corner, there came in full collision another person similarly attired.

Amongst the lower classes there is one answer, and only one, to this kind of inquiry, and it takes the shape of a counter-demand,—

"Where are *you* shoving to, I should like to know?"

Now, two questions and no answer create a very awkward state of things. It is difficult to see how a discussion can go on under such circumstances. There is immediately a tendency to cease talking, and come to something more decisive.

"I am a good mind to take that bag of yours," said the last speaker, in allusion to an apparently weighty receptacle carried by the first, "and beat you about the head with it."

Upon this threat, the bearer of the bag made a feint of assaulting his opponent, who, in turn, menacingly advanced, when—the bag was laid on the path, and its owner fled as fast as his legs could carry him. The other man looked in astonishment, and then, waxing valiant at sight of the retreating enemy, went in pursuit. But he was soon tired, and he returned to the spot, buoyant but breathless.

His eye fell on the bag. He passed his hand over its exterior, and then staggered back against the railings, and clung to them for support.

For it *is* a startling thing, reader, when you take up a blue bag dropped by a stranger in the street, to hear issuing from it a cry which, for all the world, says, "Here's a new-born baby. Oh, do please let me out, I'm being suffocated. Oh, now, pray make haste!"

It was just dark, and there was no one in the street. The alarmed discoverer hesitated for a moment, and then quietly put down the bag—(people don't care about such a prize as a stray baby)—but in the act of doing so, he was grasped strongly by the collar. He was in

the custody of one of the few policemen who at that
time had Bramblestone under their protection.

"That's Squire Wigley's plate, or I'm a Dutchman,"
exclaimed the official, his mind preoccupied by a robbery
which had recently thrown the whole town into a state
of perturbation. "And you're bound for a trip to
furrin' shores, or Simple Simon's my name, and thàt's
all about it," he added.

"Well, Mr. Baggs, you take possession of the Squire's
plate," replied the supposed thief, "and me too, if you
like."

"What! is it you, Joe Smith?" cried the policeman,
in a tone of disappointment. "Oh! then the reward's
as far off as ever. But what's this? Mercy! there's
something more lively than plate in that bag. Where
did you get it from?"

An explanation was afforded. The mouth of the bag
was opened, and then the pair made at once for the
workhouse at the end of the town. There there was
drawn forth, from its most uncomfortable quarters, a
fine, healthy infant, which screamed with an energy,
as though it were denouncing the barbarity with which
it had been treated.

Well, well, why all this detail, tedious and dull? I
must own, reader, the foregoing might have been told
in a fifth of the space. But then, you see, it would
never do to tell our tales in fashion as we would write
despatches. I might have embodied it in the following
dozen or so of words :—"A man, carrying a blue bag

containing a baby, dropped it one night in Bramblestone, and ran away. The infant was carried to the
workhouse." Very interesting this would have been,
would it not? But have patience. I have not three
volumes before me, so I am not about to acquaint you
with all the minutiæ of the poor little morsel's life. I
dash away twelve years in a single line, and show you
now a great, rough, sturdy boy, the horror of the parish
authorities, for he eats every morsel of his allowance,
and would ask for more, if there were the least chance
of good resulting.

He has been named Bartholomew Bramblestone, and
there he is, one afternoon, in the workhouse yard, playing with the other luckless lads, and in violence and
coarseness he exceeds them all. He is a very tyrant
among them. There are tyrants everywhere—even in
paupers' schools.

As this boy is a tyrant over his companions, so is the
master of the school a tyrant over the lads. They are
not likely, under any circumstances, to give him much
of their love—the air of a paupers' school is not favour-
able to affection, the plant don't grow well there by any
means—so, perhaps, he thinks he may as well have
their hatred. Well, whatever he may think, their
hatred he has, and in right good measure.

See him stalk down the workhouse yard, scowling
and scolding. The boys scud away in all directions;
but one comes within reach of the master's cane.

"There," observes the humane functionary, cutting

at the luckless wight with the full strength of his arm, " there's something for yourself; keep it, and be grate_ ful;" and then he added some odd words, very odd words, which he heard again on an after-day : *" And now go and dance a hornpipe on your mother's tomb-stone."*

While yet a dismal yell floated through the air, some visitors arrived at the workhouse, and were shown in to the master. They were a man and woman, respectably dressed. A curious tale they told. They said they had travelled from a town many miles away, where they lived. They were husband and wife, and twelve years ago their only child had been born to them. The boy had come in a time of terrible distress. They were starving. The additional burthen was intolerable. The man had a brother, who said his wife should take charge of the infant until its mother, who was at death's door, should be recovered. He had accordingly removed it; but the parents soon learned that the wife had refused admission to the miserable infant, and that the husband had taken both it and himself somewhere, and had not returned; "And," added his lovely spouse, "if I've seen the back of him one while, I shan't break my heart, you may be very sure."

Years had passed, when the lost one reappeared. He hadn't made his fortune, for he returned in rags, and came once more to bully the luckless woman who years ago had fallen into senseless love of his black eyes and brawny frame.

But about the baby? Well, he said he had dropped it in Bramblestone parish, and no doubt it had been taken to the workhouse there.

The visitors then stated, that recently a great change had occurred in their wordly condition. A considerable sum of money had been left them. They would now be rejoiced to recover their son, and they had immediately sought him where it had been intimated he would most likely be found.

The story was an odd one. The master said he would bring the matter before the authorities, and now he would take them to the playground, to see the boy.

Anything but a pleasant sight he was just then. Still smarting from the blow he had received, his features bore a demoniac expression; and curses, absolutely curious from their ingenuity and intensity, were still issuing from him.

"That isn't him," said the woman, in an under-tone of dismay and surprise.

"He is the boy," replied the workhouse master. "Something's put him out, apparently, and as he don't see us, he's venting his spite."

The man looked at the woman, and the two turned away.

"I shan't hear anything more of them," thought the master; "one sight of the cub has been sufficient." But he was wrong.

"We are coming to live in this neighbourhood," said the man. "We shall take the vacant house just outside the town. You can now make all your inquiries as to the truth of what we have told you, and we wish the boy to be restored to us as soon as possible. When we have him, we shall probably be able to make him more like a human being than he is now."

So an investigation was forthwith instituted, and the statements of the visitors were verified. A communication was forwarded to the parties accordingly, and they set out to fetch their son.

Ah! that cruel schoolmaster, with that abominable cane! As if it were not bad enough to be in a work-house, with its degradation, its restrictions, and its short commons—without the addition of being continually switched, and for no other earthly reason than the pleasant feeling the movement imparted to the switcher's arm. That big, burly boy ground his teeth, and clenched his hands, and cursed mentally, till he was almost mad. Not a word had been said to him about his newly-found parents. The schoolmaster had heard about them, and was disgusted. He had always disliked the boy, and now that his position was about to be so greatly improved, he hated him.

It was the hour when the parents were journeying to the workhouse to receive their boy. Once more that boy and the schoolmaster's cane had come in contact. Fatigued with his amusement, the schoolmaster had seated himself on a great stone. There were several large pieces of jagged stone lying about.

" Joe," whispered the ill-used urchin to a companion,

"*I'm going to do it!*" And his face became like the whitewashed wall as he spoke.

" Mercy—now—don't yer !" was the muttered reply. But almost before it was completed, the infuriated youth had crept behind the ill-starred instructor, and hurled the stone at him with frenzied force.

" You've got it now," yelled the boy; and then he sprang, like a cat, up the wall of the yard, and was gone. The terror-stricken lads crowded round the prostrate body of the schoolmaster, from which the blood was flowing copiously.

At that moment the workhouse-master's voice was heard.

" Bartholomew Bramblestone !—send Bramblestone to me. I want him."

The parents had arrived.

PART II.

MANY years have passed, and the father and mother (Burley was their name, by-the-bye) are in Bramble-stone Workhouse. It is astonishing what a strong tendency some people have to descend (metaphorically speaking) to their mother earth: They fall into difficulties—you take them out. Almost immediately they are in them again. Again they are extricated, and propped up, and again the waves of woe suck them in more vigorously than before. The Burleys, when they came to Bramblestone, knew all the sweets of plenty, following the bitters of privation. But the sweets wouldn't stay—they were treated so badly. Good fortune wouldn't remain, she was so slighted. Follies that could have been avoided, and disasters which could not, played upon the Burleys like fire-engines on a conflagration, and the result was, the unfortunate couple, in their old age, crept into the workhouse to end their days.

Bramblestone Workhouse was a fine place now. The new Poor Law had passed, and it was the "Union" Workhouse, and was under the management of a Board of Guardians. At the time of which I am now speaking, there was a vacancy at this Board. Farmer Tosswill had had three bad crops of oats. The first brought on an illness, the second made him very bad, and the third killed him. You will find his sorrows inscribed on a tombstone, under the willow in Bramblestone churchyard.

Jonathan Smart, Esq., was elected to the vacancy in the Board of Guardians. This gentleman was a new comer to the neighbourhood, and rather a mystery. He was a bachelor, and lived by himself in a large house out of the town. Very reserved he seemed, and it was against his will that they appointed him guardian. He appeared well-off, if not absolutely rich, and the rumour was, that he had been many years in America, where he had made money.

One morning, shortly after receiving his new dignity, Mr. Smart came to the workhouse. The master attended him over the building, and into the yard. He looked

about him with a curiosity which he strove to conceal,
Suddenly a shrill cry sounded, and•the new guardian.
with a start, clutched his walking-stick.

"Is anybody being murdered?" he asked.

"Oh, no," replied the master ; "it is only Taggs, the
schoolmaster, beating one of the boys. He's grown too
fond of the fun, however. He always was a brute, and,
now he's old, he's beyond bearing. The youngsters
would murder him some day (years ago one did nearly
finish him), but he's dismissed. And now, I suppose,
he'll come into the house as a pauper. There's nothing
else for him, that I see."

"That's the man seated on the stone ?" inquired Mr.
Smart ; and the master replied affirmatively.

The new guardian caught up a huge fragment, which
lay on the ground, and, advancing to the ear of the
schoolmaster, he shouted,—

"At your old tricks, Mr. Taggs, eh ? You please remember young Bartholomew Bramblestone, whom you
sent to dance a hornpipe on his mother's tombstone."

The old man jumped, as though he had been run
through the body, and both he and the master of the
workhouse reeled back in utmost amazement.

They could not recover themselves. Mr. Smart
laughed.

"There," he said, "the murder's out now ! I meant
to have kept my secret ; but the temptation of giving
my old friend a start was too great. I'm the miserable
little foundling, who ran away twenty years ago, for

something which we won't talk about now. I managed to get on board an American ship, and, over in the new country, they've treated me well enough to enable me to come back to the old one with plenty for the rest of my days."

Poor Mr. Taggs was a picture. His astonishment, the uprising of the old hatred within him, and his intense reverence for anything in the shape of a guardian, produced a conflict of emotions that turned him purple.

The master of the workhouse was at length able to offer his sincere congratulations.

"But you don't know," he said, and then he hesitated. He hardly liked to communicate hastily the story of the Burleys. It was scarcely a pleasant one for the son to hear.

"Something disagreeable coming, I see," said Mr. Smart. "Out with it!"

Thus enjoined, the master narrated, as considerately as he could, the circumstances of the unlucky parents.

"So the poor old creatures are within these walls at this moment?" observed Mr. Smart, when the master had finished. "Well, you must tell them of my arrival, and to-morrow I will come and see them. Of course I shall remove them quickly."

The next day Mr. Smart returned, and went upstairs to the master's room.

"The old lady and gentleman" (they had become "lady and gentleman," you see, reader; yesterday they were "aged paupers") "are waiting below," said the master. "They are brimful of delight."

Mr. Smart gave a grunt, as though he were scarcely in the same happy condition.

"Ah!" he remarked. "I fancy I hear their voices. Come along!"

"Take care of that top stair!" cried the master, "it's rather awk——"

The fluctuating fortune of that ill-starred couple, reader! How it flashed out at that moment! For the well-off son to meet the poor pauper parents. Oh, no! the master's caution came too late. A slip of the foot, a heavy fall, a prolonged roll, a deep sigh, a death groan! Startling occurrences within two minutes! The old people knelt down. Something they heard, a faint whisper, sounding like "mother," and that was all.

There was great difficulty subsequently in establishing their relationship to the deceased; but it was overcome, and they were placed in possession of his property. For a little while they lived comfortably enough; but, of course, a change came. Somehow their late son had been involved in law proceedings, which, after his death, terminated disastrously, and swept away all he had left. So back came the poor people into the workhouse. One (the old man) went from it, last winter, to the church-yard.

———

"Then old Mrs. Burley is still living, Mr. Jones?"

"Yes, and a little bit of sunshine has just come to her in her last days (for she's very old now) : a distant relative has offered to take her out of the workhouse, and provide for her comfortably. She won't be an encumbrance long? What now, William—anything new?"

This inquiry was to one of the workhouse messengers, who came up at the moment.

"Old Mrs. Burley just gone off in a fit, sir."

"Ah!" remarked the Relieving Officer; "ill luck has had the last word; but she's beyond its spite now."

VII.—THE ROBBERY OF THE OUT-RELIEF MONEY.

IT will be convenient with the following narrative to relate it myself, and to adopt my own arrangement of its parts for the reasons that, in this, as in some former instances, Mr. Jones's recollections are very much intertwined with my own; and that by following this independent method, I may add somewhat to the interest of the story, which was slightly marred by Mr. Jones's peculiar style of beginning at the end, then returning to the commencement, and finishing with the middle.

PART I.

A MAN coming out of a lone house in the country, at midnight, looking furtively in all directions, then gently closing the door, and manifestly preparing for a run, cannot complain much if an unobserved witness have grave doubts of his previous doings. Assuredly, those doubts will arise, and they will deepen almost into disagreeable certainties, if the mysterious individual, when he shall have commenced his flight, shall seem encumbered by something weighty, carried beneath the large cloak which fully envelops him.

From such a house, at such an hour, a man did issue forth many years back, and he acted in the way described. But this man, though before he began to run, he strained his eyes by peering through the gloom into the distance, never saw another man who stood almost at his shoulder. Like the pickpockets in a picture of Cruikshank's, who are succeeding, with most wondrous dexterity in that which would seem to be the most difficult part of their performance—the avoiding the notice of the victim—but who, nevertheless, are being coolly watched by half-a-dozen people in the background, who are only waiting the consummation of the act to clutch the offenders ; so this worthy of whom I speak, having closed the door, and ascertained that there was no one within some yards, either to the right or left, or before him, never thought for a moment that a man might be standing in the shadow, a few inches behind him. Nevertheless, there a man was; and directly the first man made off, that second man went after him at full speed, though with rather a lurching movement.

Now, the first man was what he seemed—a burglar; the second was not what he seemed—for whereas from his soiled attire, and haggard and dissolute appearance, you would have judged him a member of the common riff-raff—he was, really, the son of a most respectable man, and, for all laudable purposes, had money enough and to spare.

The thief, greatly startled at finding himself pursued, stopped short, threw something at his pursuer, and was gone like lightning.

The missile was a small, but heavy bag, which striking the pursuer in the chest, laid him prostrate. He rose with some difficulty, grasped the bag, and, leaning against a post, began to examine its contents.

It was not quite an easy matter, for the miserable being was drunk, and the untying the stout cord round the neck of the bag was a terribly arduous operation. However, it seemed, when completed, to bring its re- ward; for the watery eyes glistened when the hand, which had been hastily inserted, withdrew with abun- dance of gold coin. Looking stealthily round, the young man replaced the sovereigns, and clumsily retied the bag. This done, he seemed to hold debate with himself. I don't know the nature of his inward rea- soning; it was not very sound, we may be sure. The arguments of a drunken man, whether worked only in his own mind, or expressed to the world, cannot be worth much; and in this particular instance I am inclined to think they were positively abominable. But this is only fancy. Very likely the drunken creature didn't argue at all—the light of reason could have shone out but very little in that befogged, benighted brain. One re- solve was clearly taken—to go. So the bag was thrust into a very capacious coat pocket (almost destroying, by its weight, the owner's equilibrium), and the luckless illustration of the evil of late hours, and bad brandy and water, jogged towards the neighbouring town.

PART II.

It is not pleasant to be waked suddenly out of your first sleep; and the annoyance is increased, when you

G

have a bad cold in your head.   When Mrs. Jones, the wife of the Relieving Officer of Bramblestone, stirred him up vigorously one night with the intimation the house was on fire, Mr. Jones was neither alarmed nor grateful, but wroth.

"Nonsense, Mary."   (*A snore.*)

"Nonsense! my dear.   Mercy on me—don't you hear the people calling us ?   There's a great mob round the house, I'm sure."

This was rather a stretch of imagination ; for I verily believe that, situated where it was, Mr. Jones's house, and all that it contained, might have been reduced to ashes, with scarcely a person being the wiser until after the event.   However, Mr. Jones roused himself, and looked out of window.   One man there undoubtedly was, just underneath, bawling out for Mr. Jones, with an energy which almost excused Mrs. Jones's suggestion of a mob.

"Who in the world can it be ?" wondered the Relieving Officer.   "I'll open the window."

"No, pray don't," interposed Mrs. Jones, "you'll catch your death o' cold !   Who are you, and what do you want ?" she screamed, with all her might, rapping at the window.

"Want! botheration !" cried a gruff voice.   "I want Mr. Jones to go immediately to the Widow Worley, in the cottage by the town.   The poor creature is literally dying from disease and want of necessaries.   There's not a moment to be lost.   Her case ought to have been seen to before."

"Who is it speaks?" shouted Mr. Jones.

"Confound it, I'm Mr. Brandley, the guardian," was the reply. "Surely my having a bit of a cold ought not to prevent you recognizing my voice, even if the snow hides my body. There! pray be quick. See me in the morning, and tell me about the poor thing."

And away went a black figure, the outline of which could just be seen from the window.

"Now, upon my word, this is too bad," moaned the afflicted Relieving Officer. "It's no use my going to the old woman; that brute of a son of her's will never let me in. And to go that distance, at this time of night, and in this snow-storm, and all certainly to no purpose —why——"

"The man's a horrid Pagan," interrupted Mrs. Jones, who did not care greatly about the appropriateness of her description, so long as she conceived it to be of a highly unfavourable character.

"And yet I suppose I must go," reflected the oppressed official; "there'll be—a-tisha!—no end of—a-tisha!—at the—a-tisha!—Board, if I don't—a-tisha!"

So, sneezing every three minutes, Mr. Jones scrambled on his clothing.

"There's one thing consoles me," he said, as he was starting, " the arbitrary fellow seemed to have quite as bad a cold as mine. I shouldn't have known his voice in the least. Good-night, Mary; get into bed again, as fast as you can, or you'll catch a dreadful—a-tisha—a-tisha!—Mercy on me!—a-tisha! O dear!"

And the door shut, and remarking, with pleasure, the cessation of the snow, at all events, the obedient Relieving Officer went on his errand.

It took him quite a quarter of an hour to reach the Widow Worley's cottage. As he drew near to it, he perceived the light of a great fire in the sitting-room (don't suppose I mean a parlour, reader; I mean a little slip not much bigger than a large pig-stye, separated from two other little slips, which were bedrooms), which, at that time of night, surprised him. He approached, and rapped at the door. Receiving no answer, he knocked again loudly.

"I don't know who it is that's knocking," roared a gruff voice within; "but I tell ye this—if ye knock a third time, I'll drag ye in, and put ye into my copper here, and out ye'll not come till ye're as soft as a floury pertaty."

"I'm Mr. Jones, the Relieving Officer," cried that official, "and I'm sent by Mr. Brandley, the guardian, to see after your mother's condition."

"It's I that's seeing after the old woman's condition, and I don't want no help," was the reply.

"But don't you want a nurse?"

"It's I that's nurse, and cook, and doctor," answered the same voice; "and it's I that'll be the death of ye, in another moment, if ye don't tramp; so now, march!"

"What is the matter with your mother?" inquired Mr. Jones.

"Well, it's the typhus; there now!"

Mr. Jones shivered.

"Mr. Brandley told me she was in want," he said.

"I know nothing of Mr. Brandley, and she has plenty. Now, *are* you goin' ?"

"Curious," thought Mr. Jones. "But it's no good staying, to get my head broken by that brutal giant." And he hastened home.

He was surprised to find the door of his house unfastened, and still more surprised, when he pushed it open to be encountered by a red-hot poker, thrust within an inch of his nose by his own dear wife.

"Murder ! — Robbery ! — Thieves !" shrieked Mrs. Jones, brandishing her formidable weapon, and then dropping both it and her cries, on recognizing her husband.

Mr. Jones divined the truth in a moment.

"What have they taken, Mary ?" he asked.

"It's not 'they,' but 'he,'" answered Mrs. Jones ; "for there was but one of them. He must have broken in directly after you'd gone ; for in five minutes the villain was in my room, threatening me. But now, the odd thing is, I miss nothing. He didn't stay more than a minute."

The Relieving Officer said not a word ; but sprung up stairs, his wife following him. He hunted in a corner, and then looked up despairingly.

"It's gone," he groaned.

"Why, there was nothing there," said his surprised wife.

"There was, indeed," was the reply. "There was seventy pounds there, Mary, in a bag,—all the out-relief money for to-morrow. There was something the matter with the lock of the iron safe in the office, and I brought the money home for security. Oh, Mary! I shall have to make it good. This has been a very bad night for me."

There was not much sleep for the luckless pair that night. The first thing next morning Mr. Jones went to Mr. Brandley. On his return, he said,—

"Just as I had been thinking, Mary; that must have been a regular plot last night. Mr. Brandley wasn't out of his bed. I have a great difficulty in seeing him: brute as he always is, he is something like a demon this morning. His son, who only returned from sea a week ago, and who certainly seems a thorough scape-grace, has been hurt in some brawl so severely, that it is doubtful whether he survives, and the house is in confusion. But this much the father was pleased to insinuate, that he didn't believe a word about the robbery, and that, in any case, he was determined, so far as his influence extended (and you know his power, Mary), I should be compelled to restore the money."

"Then he's a mean brute, and story-teller—a down-right, shocking Brahmin!" said Mrs. Jones, entertaining a vague notion that by the latter appellation she had visited Mr. Brandley with the heaviest conceivable denunciation.

The story was noised abroad; and at the weekly meeting of the guardians next day there was a very full attendance. There being no money, the unfortunate paupers had not, of course, been paid, and the mingled bewailing and abuse with which the air was filled sounded by no means pleasantly.

Directly after the reading of the minutes of the last meeting, Mr. Brandley said,—

"I have come down here out of a sick bed, and I have left behind me an almost dying son, to know why these poor people are not paid. I have heard some trumpery story about money being improperly—("Now, pray, Brandley, pray," interposed the Chairman, but without effect)—I say, improperly withdrawn from the office, and, without sufficient reason, lodged in the Relieving Officer's house; and then I'm told some cock-and-bull tale, with which my name is impertinently mixed up, as to the Relieving Officer having been led away by a fictitious application, in the middle of the night, and his house being robbed of this bag (and, mind you, of this bag only) during his absence. Now, gentlemen, you may do what you please; but I'm not going to forget my duty. I'll not mince matters; I accuse that man, Mr. Jones—"

"Upon my word, Mr. Brandley," again interposed the Chairman, Mr. Eardley, "I must stop you."

"You will *not* stop me, sir," replied the excited guardian, "unless you choose to order the porter to put me out by the shoulders. I shall—"

Here the guardians rose in a body, and a perfect hubbub ensued.

"Hark to those cries outside!" shouted Mr. Brandley. "Many a poor creature there is, I daresay, well-nigh starving at this moment, and all because—"

"But, my good friend," said the Chairman, "you go along at such a steam-engine pace. The first thing is to hear from Mr. Jones a distinct account. Bless my soul!" he exclaimed, "those people are making an uproar, sure enough."

The noise outside was, indeed, dreadful. There seemed smart scuffling going on, and cries of "murder" were very audible. The guardians fidgetted considerably in their seats.

"Now, look you!" cried Mr. Brandley, "you believe what you like, all of you" (and he looked round contemptuously); "but I say, that until some other man shall make his appearance with the money, I believe Mr. Jones to be——"

Who was this who, after having apparently overcome strong opposition without, came tumbling into the room and rushed to table? A young man he was, yet pale and shrunken, as by old age; there was "early grave" upon his features, stamped there plainly and distinctly, so that none could fail to see it. He threw upon the table a small but heavy bag, and the chink of gold told its contents.

"There it is," he said, in something of an exulting tone. "Don't stare, father. They say I'm going to

die. Then let me, at all events, get *that* off my conscience. Last night, as I was coming home, I saw a
man run out of a house. I guessed what he'd been
about, and followed him, and he threw that at me
(giving me the blow that has well-nigh finished me),
and escaped. And when I saw what was in the bag,
I meant to keep it; I wanted it——"

"You scoundrel, you idiot!" shouted the astounded
father. "What are you talking about?"

"What's the good of it to a man who's going to die?
I thought of this half-an-hour ago, and I said, 'I'll go
down, and give it up myself before them all.' And I've
come. I let no one prevent me. I've had a fight for it;
but I've come, and there——"

But before he had finished the sentence, his father had
clutched him, and strove to force him from the room.
A wild cry, and a stream of blood issuing from the
mouth of the young man, showed that he had broken a
blood vessel, and the father fell back, horrified. The
board adjourned. Mr. Brandley never came again.

I am pleased at being able to bring in a little sunshine
at the close of this narrative. Young Brandley did *not*
die. He recovered, and he positively blessed the circumstance which led to his making the moral effort
above described. It was the commencement of right
doing; it was the turn of thought; it was the entrance
of light into a heart where before all had been darkness; and Brandley, the son, still lives, a prosperous,
and upright, and benevolent man.

VIII.—BUBBLE FOR GUARDIAN.

"Look at that, sir," said Mr. Jones to me, one morning, "that is vexing, is it not?"

He handed me a local newspaper, and pointed to the following advertisement:—

"BRAMBLESTONE PARISH.

"ELECTION OF GUARDIANS.

"Electors, I offer you my services. My sentiments on all main questions are well known to you. You are thoroughly acquainted with my views on the present cost of washing the workhouse towels, and I can assure you that give way on the subject of frills to the women's nightcaps, I never will. I shall be duly nominated at the proper time, and, if opposed, I shall place my hand on my heart, and rely on you.

"I am, your devoted servant,

"BARTHOLOMEW BUBBLE."

"Place his hand on his head, and call for a keeper, would be the more natural action, Mr. Jones," I observed. "It certainly is a remarkable effusion. Is the little man crazed?"

"Well, the fact is, his wife more than hints that he is," replied the Relieving Officer; "but I don't believe myself, there's anything the matter with him beyond silliness. However, it's a nuisance to have such a man at the board."

"But you don't mean to say that he will be actually elected?"

"Oh, he is safe to be. He will be nominated, and there will be no opposition. Having for years been in the employ of Lord Longbill, no one will think of opposing him. His Lordship has, in all probability, suggested to him this step. Very vexing, very vexing, indeed!"

And Mr. Jones put the paper in his pocket with a savage air, as though he should like to have Mr. Bubble in the stone-yard. But Mr. Jones need not have worried himself. Mr. Bubble was not fated to represent Brambleetone parish on the Board of Guardians. Trouble was in store for him. Herewith is the narrative:—

PART I.

Hush, hush! Bring only a grave and solemn spirit into this drear abode. In a wretched hut, standing rather more than a mile from the end house in the town, and equally distant from any other dwelling, an appalling deed was done. A man, bad and dangerous at all times, had been rendered by drink a very demon. He had previously committed, I may almost say, every crime of which human nature is capable, save one—murder. And now that was added. He struck down his unoffending wife, and killed her.

This was at night time. In the morning, the man

came into the town, and surrendered himself to the
police; for the magnitude of this last crime had crushed
him. "He never thought of *murder*," he said. "There
was no quarrel between them." It was terrible, but it
was true. The blow which had scattered his victim's
brains upon the hearth-stone, had been inflicted in the
frenzy of drunkenness, almost as a joke; and its mur-
derous power only became known to him when his wife
lay dead upon the floor. *Then*, even the strong drink
within him lost its influence, and he looked down into
the gulf which had opened at his feet. He could not
fly. The tragedy of his life was. closing. He went
quietly to the prison and to the gallows.

Such an event, you may be sure, created a great sen-
sation in the neighbourhood. The first movement was
a tumultuous rush to view the hut; to scrutinize the
only partially obliterated stains upon the floor and wall;
to sit in the chair wherein sat the victim when the blow
fell; and to exchange conjectures, in an under-tone
(as though her ghost were near), upon her death
agony. Before the cottage had been quite pulled to
pieces, an order arrived from its owner peremptorily to
close it.

Now, its owner was no less a person than Lord Longbill. That his lordship should have suffered such a
miserable abode to remain on his estate was strange;
but great men sometimes hold, and reap benefit from,
odd possessions. His lordship instructed Mr. Bubble—
who managed his property of this description, and kept

the key of the cottage—to allow no more persons to inspect it, without express sanction.

But his lordship could not prevent Lady Longbill, one morning, forming the notion that she should like to see the ill-starred place. Was it so utterly strange, reader, that her ladyship should have conceived this idea? I'll venture to say, my friend, that if you and I had been living in the neighbourhood, we should have gone to the place, and examined it from top to bottom. Wherever there has been, or is, something horrible, there will both men and women be gathered. I, who am opposed to capital punishment, and shrink from seeing pain inflicted upon anything that breathes, am quite assured, that if an opportunity were afforded me, I should go to see a man hanged. I should be filled with horror; but my eyes would refuse to move from the spectacle. The truth is, anything violently strange and startling so stimulates curiosity in the vulgar, and arouses thought in the intellectual, that other emotions give way. They murmur, so to speak, but they submit.

" I really should like to see the cottage," said her Ladyship, at breakfast time. "I suppose nobody goes there now?"

"O, no; you won't be interrupted," replied Lord Longbill; "you'll have the place to yourself, unless, indeed, there's a ghost in it. They say there is, you know, and, even in the daytime, the country people won't go within half a mile of it. It's a funny fancy of your's (mind, reader, his lordship had been one of the first visitors to the hut himself); but if you are bent upon it, Bubble, in the town, will give you the key, and you can let yourself in."

So, about mid-day, Lady Longbill, having called at Mr. Bubble's and obtained the key from his wife (Mr. Bubble being absent), journeyed to the dreary dwelling. The lower window had been boarded over, to prevent persons getting or looking in, and a bar had even been placed against the upper. Lady Longbill applied the key, and opened the door with some difficulty. This done, she half resolved to retreat; but, gathering fresh courage, she advanced into the room, taking care, however, to leave the door open. Having contemplated the miserable apartment for some minutes, no doubt with much advantage, her ladyship thought she would ascend the stairs. She had just reached the top, when she heard a sound coming from below. Her ladyship's pulse, which before had travelled at the usual healthy rate of seventy beats a minute, sprung at once to one hundred. She dared not go down, but she ran to the bedroom window, and, looking out thence, she saw something which surprised her vastly. There was a man at the entrance, and she knew his face well. He had closed the door, and now he was turning the key, which her ladyship had left in the lock outside. What next did he do? Mercy! Before her ladyship could recover from her consternation, this person had turned round, and—eh?—yes—had made off as fast as his legs

could carry him. Lady Longbill was speechless. Then
an intense terror caused her to shake in every limb.
She rushed to the door. Ah! there was no stirring it.
She tried the windows. Dear me! quite useless.
Then she shrieked with all her power. Not the smallest good in the world. She exhibited hysterics. The
walls were perfectly indifferent, so she soon recovered.
An hour, two hours, four hours passed; still her ladyship remained imprisoned. It grew dusk. She thought
perhaps she should die of fright; but then she determined to do her very best to live, that she might bring
condign punishment on the scoundrel who had caused
her sufferings.

PART II.

Mr. and Mrs. Bubble sat at breakfast.

"My dear," said the latter, "I've a great fancy to
see the room where the murder was committed. Nobody goes near the place now, so I should not be seen."

"Oh, it's shut up, you know," replied Mr. Bubble;
"and it's a wretched hole. You're better away, Lucy."

"Where shall I find the key?" asked the lady, not
caring to notice the opposition.

"In the usual place," he answered, shortly. "I must
say I think you are foolish to go."

"Now, pray, my dear, you let me take care of myself. There is nobody in the place who will eat me, is
there?"

"Certainly not," promptly replied her husband,

thinking what a ferocious cannibal must be found to
devour Mrs. Bubble, who was "a fine woman," at the
age of sixty. "Still, as there is nothing to see, you're
better away."

"Why in the world shouldn't I go?" exclaimed Mrs.
Bubble. "Mrs. Drum and Mrs. Tissiman went the
other day."

"I didn't see them, my dear."

"You are so near-sighted, my love, you see nobody."

"I see all I want to see, Lucy. Well, have your
own way. Go, by all means. Beware of the ghost!"

"Nonsense! there's no ghost will face me, I know,"
said Mrs. Bubble. And Mr. Bubble assented, with an
inward sigh; for he thought, if he knew of one, how
quickly he'd hire him to do battle with his beloved
spouse in his behalf. And the little man departed on
his daily business.

In the afternoon of that day, Mr. Jones, the Relieving
Officer, called on Mrs. Bubble. Now, no scandal! The
visit was a kindly-intentioned one, and had reference
solely to Mr. Bubble; for that diminutive gentleman
was seeking to be guardian of the poor of his parish,
and, for his own sake, and for the sake of the poor,
quite as much as for Mr. Jones's sake, it was desirable
to dissuade him from his purpose. Now all in the
parish knew that the way to turn the key upon Mr.
Bubble—if one may be excused the phrase—was to
hint to his dear wife that he had too much freedom. So
the Relieving Officer determined to see the strong-minded

lady, and gently lead her thoughts in the proper direction.

"You see, Mrs. Bubble," observed Mr. Jones, in his most agreeable style, "I am so sure the excitement would be too much for Mr. Bubble. You have no idea of the mental strain to which a Guardian is subjected."

"Ah, then he's not fit for the office," said Mrs. Bubble, shaking her head. "His mind will bear no strain, that I'm quite sure of. But I shouldn't have thought that was wanted for a Guardian. It's easy enough to order the paupers to work, and to send 'em to prison, isn't it?"

"Certainly," replied Mr. Jones, thinking within himself how beloved Mrs. Bubble would have been as a Guardian; "but then there are the debates."

"The debates?"

"Yes, the solemn discussions at the Board—long speeches — difficult questions — the washing towels—frills to the nightcaps."

"True; I see. No, I'm afraid he's not equal to those things. Do you know, I'm very anxious about him even now."

"Indeed! Is Mr. Bubble unwell?"

"Too much upon the brain," answered Mrs. Bubble, in a tremulous whisper.

"Bless me!" exclaimed Mr. Jones, with an air of deep sympathy. "Well, Mr. Bubble is one of the last persons I should have suspected to be labouring under an overloaded brain."

H

"Gets very excited at times," said Mrs. Bubble, in a melancholy tone; "contradicts me now and then."

"Does he, indeed!" exclaimed the Relieving Officer, deeply touched at this convincing evidence of Mr. Bubble's weakened intellect. "He doesn't often manifest his—his lunacy, does he?"

"Not often—no," replied the lady. "When he does I fix my eye upon him in this way, and it quiets him at once."

"Ah, yes, I can understand it would," said Mr. Jones. —("Nothing *could* follow that look but a sound beating with the poker," he thought to himself.)—"Well, now, you see, I've taken the liberty of speaking on this subject, because I do think, if Mr. Bubble had rather more consulted you, that—"

"Yes," interrupted Mrs. Bubble, "he was precipitate —he *is* rash at times. I will—oh, there he is!" and Mr. Bubble's usual knock (a very loud one—little men generally give loud knocks, I fancy) sounded through the house.

They were sitting in the front parlour, which opened into the back by folding doors, these doors being all but closed. They heard Mr. Bubble enter the back room, seat himself on the sofa, and enjoy a hearty giggle.

Mrs. Bubble looked at Mr. Jones in the utmost amazement. The chuckling continued, now rising into a broad laugh, now sinking into a gasping, choking sound, as though the joke would make an end of the laughter before it had done with him. The sofa creaked and groaned under the violent motion of the little man's person.

Mrs. Bubble rose, and with a very pale face, whispered in Mr. Jones's ear, " It's come at last—I should say, it's gone—quite gone."

"What's come—what's gone?" inquired Mr. Jones, likewise whispering.

" The fit's come, and the mind's gone," muttered Mrs. Bubble. "Mercy! what's that? He's beginning to talk!"

So he was. Mr. Jones peeped through the keyhole, and there he saw the diminutive gentleman, rolling his head and lifting up his hands, while tears from laughter ran down his cheeks.

" It was *so* prime," he giggled ; "there she went, so daintily, daintily," (and here Mr. Bubble imitated the walking of a fine lady), "and in she pops—he, he, he, he, he, he!" and down went the small body on the sofa, its owner being again threatened with suffocation from suppressed laughter.

("I'd better send for a doctor," whispered Mrs. Bubble to Mr. Jones. " O my poor Bartholomew!"

"Hush! wait a bit," answered the Relieving Officer. "Listen, he's saying something more.")

" *I* saw her," resumed Mr. Bubble; "I'm not so blind but I knew her red shawl a long way off."

("Eh! why he's talking of me," muttered Mrs. Bubble, still more interested.)

"Then I go creepy, creepy, and then—eh, wuick," and

Mr. Bubble made a sharp sound with his thumb and forefinger—"Oh, how she did squeal, squeal, squeal! I heard her half a mile off. Oh, it's the finest bit of fun I've known in all my days;" and up went the palms again, and over rolled the little body on the sofa, finally resting with its head downwards on the cushion.

Mr. Jones began to think that the part he and Mrs. Bubble were playing ought to be concluded.

"Let's open the door," he whispered.

"Very well," was the reply. Mrs. Bubble in a moment had clasped her spouse in a powerful embrace.

"My Barty, my Barty," she was beginning to exclaim (taking care to pinion his arms), when Mr. Bubble, looking up, uttered a yell so terrific, that Mrs. Bubble, in her surprise, released him.

"*You* here!" he shouted; " why—eh—why—who —who let you out?"

"There, there, Barty," replied Mrs. Bubble soothingly ("They always think other people are mad, not themselves, "she muttered to Mr. Jones): "now, dearey, go into the little room upstairs just for the present, will you? nobody shall have the key but me; do, dearey."

At this affectionately-intentioned speech, Mr. Bubble rubbed his head, stared very hard at Mrs. Bubble, and then, turning to Mr. Jones, said,—

"Jones, what's all this? I think I must be going out of my senses."

Mr. Jones himself felt rather bewildered, and made no reply.

All further wondering was cut short by the entrance of an unexpected visitor, whose knock had been unnoticed in the confusion.

"I beg pardon," cried Lord Longbill, "for coming in so abruptly, but has Lady Longbill been here to-day? She had a fancy this morning for seeing the scene of that dreadful tragedy, and started several hours ago. I cannot think what has become of her."

"Her Ladyship called here quite early," replied Mrs. Bubble, "and took the key of the cottage, and——oh! I'm a dead woman—fetch me my bonnet!"

This singular self-interruption in the current of Mrs. Bubble's reply was occasioned by a very alarming movement on the part of Mr. Bubble, who suddenly sprang forward (nearly knocking his good wife, who "had her eye upon him," into the fireplace), dashed past Lord Longbill, and was out of the house in an instant.

"Oh, my Lord, my Lord!" screamed the afflicted wife, "he's gone raving mad! Oh, let us go after him! Oh, come along!"

Completely taken by surprise, his Lordship followed Mrs. Bubble (who did not wait for the bonnet) and Mr. Jones into the street.

"There he is," cried Mr. Jones; and the party could just descry Mr. Bubble some distance off, running like a dog that has robbed the "meatman."

"After him," cried his Lordship, who was a jovial, hearty spirit; and away went the three pursuers, helter-skelter, up the main street in Bramblestone.

Well, it *was* an odd sight for Bramblestone to see Mr. Bubble tearing along, as though for the bare life, without any hat, his eyes glaring, and almost foaming at the mouth; and then, some little distance behind him, to see Mrs. Bubble without a bonnet, Lord Longbill, and Mr. Jones making after him, like the police after a pickpocket. The people came to their doors, and stared in amazement, and some of them joined in pursuit. By the time the pursuers had quitted the town, their number had increased to quite a mob, and the shouts were terrific.

Still, Mr. Bubble kept ahead. Over stiles and hedges he went, and over stiles and hedges went the hunters and huntresses, until the unfortunate object of pursuit had reached the well-known cottage. There he stopped, and by the time the mob had come up, Lady Longbill stood beside him.

Astonishment was in every face. Lady Longbill spoke first :—

"Lord Longbill," said her Ladyship, in an excited tone, "I don't know whether this man is mad, or drunk, or foolish; but you will not hesitate to order him immediately into custody, when I tell you that by him I have been imprisoned five hours in that wretched place. While I was in there, he stole up and locked me in. I saw him, though he doubtless did not know it."

"My Lady, my Lady," implored the poor little man, who would have dropped on his knee, but it was so very muddy just there; "pray forgive me   I did not know

it was you, indeed I did not. I thought I was
playing just a little innocent trick upon my good lady.
She said she was going, and I was mistak—"

Alas! poor Mr. Bubble. In asking to turn aside the
flood of Lady Longbill's wrath he had unwittingly set in
motion the overwhelming lava of his wife's indignation.
Mrs. Bubble heard his excuse, and—

"What, sir! what, Mr. Bubble!" she exclaimed ma-
jestically and unnaturally. "What, you odious creature!
What, you insulting wretch!" she screamed in an angry-
cook style, and most naturally, "a trick upon *me!* You
thought to lock me in! Oh—ah—yes. I see now—
you were quite in your senses when you were chuckling
in the back parlour. Yes, yes! you were laughing at me.
O-o-o-o-o-h!"

Now, when "a fine woman" makes that noise at a very
small man, it behoves the latter to think what may
come next. This Mr. Bubble did, and the result was
he scampered back towards the town like a racehorse.

Again the cry arose, "After him— after him!" and
again we started, the whole posse of us (except Lord and
Lady Longbill) in hot pursuit. On went the little man,
and on we went too, over gates and through ditches, and
the shouts were deafening. I believe the pursuers
would have been beaten,—I do think they would,—but
just as we entered the town, there emerged from a cottage, full in Mr. Bubble's path, a sweep with a great
bag of soot. Things do sometimes happen at most un-

toward moments. Mr. Bubble could not stop himself.
In an instant, the sweep, Mr. Bubble, and the soot-bag
were cuddling one another on the ground.

———

"Who have they nominated for Guardian of Bramblestone, Mr. Jones?"

"A very respectable man, sir; Mr. Smithy, the muffin and crumpet maker."

———

IX.—THE STEP-MOTHER.

THAT frequent source of trouble, a second marriage,
had cast its shadow over Burleigh Grange. There were
many who had prophesied evil, should Mr. Marley
marry Widow Stelvill, and evil had come to pass. For
there was a son by Mr. Marley's former wife,—a self-
willed, domineering lad, now fifteen years of age; and
to him, of course, this second marriage was odious in
the last degree.

"Don't do it, father; I say she'll kill you," urged
the boy.

Mr. Marley smiled, and patted his son's head, saying,—

"Nonsense, Harry! Mrs. Stelvill will kill neither
of us. She will be a good wife to me, and to you a
second mother."

The boy made no reply to his father. He ran out
and made one to the woods wherein he rambled, and it

was one which I cannot record, so full was it of sinful hate, expressed in language coarse and shocking.

Love, they say, is blind; it certainly is sometimes mad. It was notorious that Mrs. Stelvill and her late husband had led a very unhappy life. The deceased had left his wife and his quarrels only three years after the wedding. "Worn out," said the sympathizing villagers. "Downright murdered!" openly asserted not a few of the better class. And yet, with this character, Mr. Marley (a quiet, spiritless man himself) was going to marry the widow. What did he see in her so fascinating? Ah, my friend, how many a man after marriage has winced at the thought of this question being buzzed about concerning his own case. But never mind, don't be cast down over it. Remember we are all alike. How Jones came to fall in love when he did it, the consequences looming in the distance—what is the use of attempting to discuss these questions with the demented individual? He'll give in at once to all your reasoning; he'll see his folly: he'll break the trammels without delay; and, when your back is turned, he'll twist and twirl the net around him more completely than ever, and, when you come to congratulate him on his freedom, you find him—married.

Six months had not expired before Mr. Marley had recovered his senses, and had been to see that the family vault was in a good state of repair. For the deceased Stelvill, losing flesh and strength daily, was a gloomy vision ever present to his mind. How he (Marley) had

laughed at Stelvill, had tried to cheer him up, had
pointed out to him his good fortune in possessing such a
treasure of a wife; how Stelvill (when his wife was not
present) had smiled a sickly smile, and answered, " No
one could know Henrietta's full worth except her husband;" and how Stelvill wasted away, until there was
scarcely anything of him left to put in his coffin—these
reminiscences were constantly staring the second husband in the face, and he speculated on the probability
of a third wedding between a third delusionist and a
certain Widow Marley.

Besides a host of vague troubles in connection with
his dear wife, which Mr. Marley would have been puzzled exactly to specify, but which realized to his mind the
condition of a canary bird, with its eyes put out, con-
fined in a cage, allowing simply of its hopping from its
perch on to the floor, and from the floor to its perch again,
there was one great grievance almost always present,
and at which Mr. Marley shuddered :—the spirit of the
dead wife had been imparted to her son. Imperious and
passionate, Harry Marley was just what his mother had
been. With a deep, devoted affection, towering above
all her faults of temper, the late Mrs. Marley had loved
her husband; with equal warmth and vehemence Harry
Marley loved his father. Hence battles repeated and
terrible ensued between the dead wife's unworthy suc-
cessor and the dead wife's child.

"I tell you I'll not bear it—I will not! Now mind,
I say it for the last time !" Mrs. Marley would exclaim,

while her husband would roll on the sofa, and groan.
"If that boy dares to address me again in the way he's
now done, he shall be put out of doors by the footman."

"Father, father, how can you let her treat us all so ?"
appealed the youth, when the tyrant had departed. "If
things are to go on like this, I'll beg my bread rather
than stop here."

"Why not have sent the boy away ?" asks the reader.
For these reasons. First, he positively refused to go,
having an undefined notion that if he ever lost sight of
his father, he should not see him again. Secondly, because his father really could not bring himself to part
with him ; the boy's dread of final separation was in his
mind too ; so Mr. Marley hoped and tried to make peace
between the combatants, and, with not an uncommon
result, he aggravated their enmity to a degree that was
quite astonishing.

At length, when they had quarrelled to the full extent that words would allow, they came to fisticuffs.
Thus arose the climax.

Some small matters (it don't need a great one, when
people are itching for an encounter) had once again
raised a contest between the parties. They were alone,
and therefore, being unchecked by the cry of shame,
which would have arisen from witnesses, they both
"forgot themselves," to use the common phrase, in manner they had never done before. Now, there is a point
where words must stop. People must feel they have
used them to the utmost, and, if the contest is to be

continued, some new weapons must be had recourse to.
Abuse between Mrs. Marley and her stepson could no
further go; so the disputants fell to blows. It was a
bad change for the lady. She, indeed, began boldly, by
hurling at Harry an inkstand, which, had it struck him,
would have put him *hors de combat;* but he dodged
aside, and it smashed a mirror. Then, in retaliation,
the youth seized his father's heavy walking-stick, which
stood handy, and belaboured his good step-mother with
all his might.

She deserved it, but I don't defend the act, reader;
for Harry was now sixteen, and to strike a woman as
he did, with all the power of a vigorous arm, was a
brutal proceeding. Mrs. Marley screamed until the
house rung again, and the first person to enter the room
was Mr. Marley.

The moment was unpropitious for Harry. Mr. Marley
did not see the broken inkstand in the corner, and he did
see the strong boy beating with a great stick the com-
paratively weak woman. For the instant, he was much
roused, and seizing the youth with no gentle hand, he
cast him on the ground, reproaching him bitterly the
while.

My friend, if you should have to fight a battle with
your fists, or with your tongue, or, indeed, with any weapon, pray do try and keep your perception clear, and your
temper cool. It is a thing I cannot possibly accomplish
myself; but never mind, the advice is undeniable notwithstanding. If Master Harry had been patient instead
of passionate, quietly determined instead of violently

headstrong, he might have again turned the tide in his favour, and come off victorious. As it was, he completed his own defeat, by heaping on his father the most furious invectives, and then he rushed from the room.

"I hope you've seen and heard enough *now*," burst forth Mrs. Marley. "It's a mercy I'm still living."

"He must leave the house certainly," remarked Mr. Marley, much cast down. "He'd better go at once. Any more of this work will drive me mad. I'll write a note to my brother, in London, asking him to take charge of the boy for awhile. Harry will leave with it this afternoon."

The note was accordingly written, and Mr. Marley handed it, with several bank notes enclosed in an envelope, to Mrs. Marley, saying,—

"See him, please, Henrietta, and give him these, telling him I wish him to go by the afternoon coach, and, before he goes, I will speak to him in the library."

Having learned that Master Harry was in the grounds, Mrs. Marley sought and found him there.

"Your father desires you will leave for London by the afternoon coach," she said, "and there is money for your journey, and to enable you to live for three months, at least," she added, handing the envelope containing the bank notes.

Harry was so surprised, that he took the envelope mechanically, and said nothing.

"You will find plenty of places in London, where you can stay cheaply," resumed Mrs. Marley. "At the end of two months, you will write your father, giving a minute account of yourself up to that date, and, if it should be satisfactory, more money will be sent you, not otherwise."

"I will see my father," interposed the boy, abruptly.

"You will not," was the peremptory reply. "His order is, that you go at once to the inn, and await the coach, and your luggage will be sent you there."

Angry as the boy was against his father, he would not persevere in his demand to see him. With a very audible malediction, he turned away, and went to the inn, as directed. Thither, in half-an hour, came his luggage; then the London coach arrived, and bore him from his home, for the first time in his life.

Mrs. Marley slowly retraced her steps to the house.

"A boy like that," she muttered, "with a round sum in his pocket, running loose in London—what are the chances of his turning up again? When the money's gone, will he ever bring himself to tell what he's done with it, in order to get more? No, no. It may require a little skill, but I think I've got rid of you, young sir. I think I have. We shall see."

"I've done what you wished," said Mrs. Marley, entering the dining-room; "but he flatly refuses seeing you; so I've requested him to wait the coach at the inn, and his packages shall be sent him."

"Foolish boy!" exclaimed Mr. Marley. "Then I must go to him."

But his wife stood before him.

"Shame, shame!" she cried. "After the scene this

morning, and after this fresh burst of petulance, to go to him in such a way!"

"Yes; I believe you are right," sighed the father. "Send the things, and let him go. He will soon repent."

Matters turned out pretty nearly as Mrs. Marley anticipated. First, there was great wonderment at no news of Harry's arrival in town. Then there was greater at the startling information of his never having reached his uncle's. Inquiries were set on foot, but without success. At length, in about a month's time, there came a letter from him to his father, stating, very shortly, that he could not possibly wait longer; all his money was gone, and he must have some more. As to his mode of living during the month, he must decline saying anything about it.

This letter was a disagreeable surprise to Mrs. Marley, but it did not mar her plans. Mr. Marley was puzzled by some parts of the letter, but the general construction he put upon it was, that Harry had openly thrown off all restraint and authority, and would pursue any course his perverse will suggested. Mr. Marley was ill at the time, or he would have gone to London (or, rather, would have attempted to go, for his wife would certainly have stopped him), to see the headstrong youth. He wrote him such a letter as might be expected, enclosing him money, and begging him to come to Burleigh Grange without delay.

As to this letter, better say, shortly, without explanation, "it didn't go."

A brief retrospect—Harry arrived, for the first time,
in London. He was now a strong, well-grown youth,
full of health, and a great deal too full of spirit. He
was disgusted and angry, even to recklessness. And he
had in his pocket the thirty pounds given him by his
father, and thirty pounds of his own, which he had saved.
Now there's a nice combination of circumstances for the
boy's welfare, friend reader. Let me consider—what
would most likely ensue? There scarcely could be but
one train of consequences. Harry Marley soon made acquaintances, soon found out "the pleasures of London,"
soon sunk into disgrace and difficulty. And it was
when his money was all but gone that he wrote home,
as we have seen. Had he written an honest letter, all
might have been well; but his consciousness of error
(ah, Mrs. Marley had well calculated there!) caused
him to adopt the ambiguous style, which still kept the
cloak over the base treatment he had received from his
step-mother. As has been intimated, no answer to his
letter reached him. Furious and desperate, he employed
the small remainder of his means in accompanying a
dissolute companion to Paris, and there a street row
soon made him acquainted with the walls of a prison.

PART II.

THE country was very pretty, and the air healthy round
Bramblestone. Numbers of invalids came there in summer time. In the large, handsomely furnished drawing-
room of a house in the outskirts lay an invalid, of whom

the doctors had said that his hour was at hand. He was afflicted with no distinct malady; but life had been oozing from him for months past.

The invalid was Mr. Marley. Since the departure of his son, twelve months ago, he had drooped daily. All efforts to discover that son had proved fruitless. Success would have cured Mr. Marley; but only failure accrued, and so the end drew near.

He had been lying on a sofa, near the fire, gazing listlessly at the huge flakes of snow descending without. "Another week," he thought, "and the snow will probably be falling on my grave." It was a dreary picture, but he looked at it steadily; for that poor, nerveless man had roused strangely when death came nigh. You may see this sometimes in dying men, and it does you good to see it. The stricken, cowering, shivering mortal, who couldn't struggle with a single worldly difficulty, braces himself up at the last, and confronts the King of Terrors with an aspect which the bravest can scarce hope to assume. The-inner spirit, of which you hardly get a glimpse in life's heyday, shines out then, and the last few minutes are the brightest and the best of the man's whole earthly existence.

In the next room stood Mrs. Marley, with her back to the fire, and her hands behind her, an attitude which well indicated the lady's character. She was as much changed, though differently, as her husband. She was now stout in an unsightly degree, and her face was highly flushed, and her eyes disagreeably glistening.

Opposite to her stood the very embodiment of timidity, the village apothecary.

"Then you think death will take place in a few hours?" observed the lady, quickly.

"Oh, dear, no," was the eager reply. "I haven't the idea of such a thing. With care and attention, we shall get round, I hope."

"Eh?" exclaimed Mrs. Marley. "Why, mercy on me! didn't you say just now he wouldn't survive the night?"

"Oh, bless me! I beg pardon—a thousand pardons. Yes, yes; you mean Mr. Marley? Ah!" and the little doctor shrugged his shoulders, and looked dismal.

"You surely couldn't think I was speaking of myself?" sharply observed Mrs. Marley. "*I'm* not dying, you know."

"Most certainly not, madam. With care, and attention, and constant—".

"Bother!" interrupted Mrs. Marley, disdainfully. "You've made me quite ill; but there, never mind; good evening."

"Good evening—I really beg—I'll send a little of the restorative essence."

"I shan't take it. Go, please."

And the little doctor hurried off, muttering to himself, "So much the better; the idea of giving a woman like that 'restorative essence.' Eugh! Prussic acid more suitable. An uncivil Amazon."

Ah! Mrs. Marley, that sharp twinge, which caused

you to put your hand to your side, and sink into a chair, should have furnished food for a little more reflection than it did, especially following the meek apothecary's blunder.

"Very odd," she muttered, after a painful gasp. "Nonsense! life isn't going out of me yet. Pshaw! Twenty years' more enjoyment, or five-and-twenty, or thirty—why not thirty?—before I need think of that old family vault, the wretched place! Oh, here comes Taverly."

There was announced, and there entered the room at the same moment, the solicitor of that name, who had come to reside in Bramblestone about a year back. He was a tall, handsome man, with great black whiskers, but not pleasant looking. His face bore usually a sullen expression, which was very disagreeable; when it exhibited a smile, the effect was decidedly worse.

The servant gone, Mrs. Marley quietly advanced upon the lawyer, and taking him by the collar, as a policeman would a thief, she drew him to the mantel-piece. Then releasing him, she said, in an under tone—

"Now, Charles, don't be a fool."

"I am not a fool," was the reply, in a subdued tone; "but as to this business, Henrietta, upon my word, I don't know what to say about it. The risk, you know, the risk is the thing."

"Charles," said Mrs. Marley, "you still keep prating about the risk. The risk is nothing. The gain is ten thousand pounds. Why, Charles Taverly, what has the

world done to you of late years, that you should have
become so craven-hearted ?   When you and I were together, years ago, I loved you for the spirit in you,
which defied everybody and everything.   Didn't we
outwit and laugh at and trample upon—aye, all the
more because we never allowed him a chance of vengeance or even of sympathy from the world, albeit he
was convinced that he was wronged—that poor, weak
creature, Stelvill ?   And .what has made you cower
before this man Marley ?   Why should you have kept
away from me all this time ?   However, I shall soon be
free again, and free with a fortune which will well repay
the waiting.   Yet this fortune must be as large as we can
make it, Charles.   The will which Marley signs to-
night must NOT give ten thousand pounds to that out-
cast thing, the son.   I must have it all.   I ?   I should
say *we*.   Much more for your sake than my own I seek
the money."

"Yes, yes, Henrietta, I know," replied Taverly, in
a matter-of-fact manner, which contrasted oddly with
Mrs. Marley's vehemence; "but I again say, remember
the risk.   Suppose Marley should take a fancy to read
the will himself; or supposing even that I read—hem
—the real will, and give him—hem—the—the *other* to
sign, and he detects the ch—, the alteration.   Suppose
he should recover, or—"

"Miserable, miserable, *miserable* coward!" interrupted
Mrs. Marley.   "Oh, Charles Taverly, go your way,
man, and I'll go mine.   Get you gone, for mercy's sake !

I am sick and ill for very loathing. Why, do you think I am as much changed as yourself? Have I no resolution? You knew me of old. Were my purposes usually thwarted? Now, in a word, are you willing to bring here to-night the two documents? As to what is required afterwards, there can be, shall be, no mishap."

"Well, I will do that much," answered Taverly, who looked dubious and uncomfortable. "And now I'd better be gone, for time presses."

"Stay a minute, I'll ring for the servant; don't let yourself out. It will seem odd."

(Well, no, Mrs. Marley, it wouldn't have mattered, for a servant's ear had been at the key-hole throughout the conversation, and that explains my being able to record it here.)

The door had scarcely closed when it was re-opened, and "Mr. Jones, the Relieving Officer," was announced, with the message that he wished very much to be allowed to say a few words.

Mrs. Marley stared in great amazement.

"Send him in."

Mr. Jones entered, bowing respectfully.

"Having heard of Mr. Marley's illness, madam," he said, "I am most unwilling to intrude; yet I have thought it my duty to make a communication, which, I fear, must be very painful."

Mrs. Marley only stared, and said, shortly—

"Go on, if you please."

"About an hour ago," resumed the Relieving Officer,

"there entered the Relief Office in this place a young man, so worn and ill, that it was sad to see him. He asked assistance, and said his name was Harry Marley."

"What of that, sir?"

"Nothing, madam, by itself; but on questioning him farther, he declared he thought he was dying, and confided to me that he was the son of a Mr. Marley, of Burleigh Grange, in Norfolk; that he had been discarded by his father, and so had fallen into this wretched condition; that he was now endeavouring to reach Burleigh Grange, but believing himself dying, he communicated these facts to me, that I might acquaint his father. I knew," added Mr. Jones, "that the gentleman he alluded to was staying in this house; but before informing the poor fellow, I deemed it better to step on here, and tell you of the painful discovery."

Mrs. Marley mused for a minute, and then replied—

"The story told you is true. You call the discovery painful. It is. A vile son, the cause of his father's mortal illness, cast out of sight, it was hoped for ever, has crept into light again, just on the eve of his father's death. You say, the wretched creature is himsel dying. I say openly, I hope he is; but whatever his condition may be, I charge you, keep him from here. If he should venture here, I'll have him struck down, as I would any avowed murderer. Keep him in custody, I say; I will defray every expense; and should he live, in a day or two proper provision shall be made for him."

"I cannot keep him in custody, madam. I have no power," replied the Relieving Officer, stiffly. "I am sorry to hear what you say. Good morning."

And Mr. Jones departed, a strong impression resting on his mind that wrong was being committed. When he reached the workhouse, he communicated to the sufferer the whole story.

It was nearly dark as a bowed, attenuated figure stumbled forth from Bramblestone Workhouse, and began to wend its way into the open country. There were very few persons to see it, or alarmed observation would have been drawn to its frequent action of raising its fist against some imaginary foe, and shaking it vindictively. It rolled, and staggered, and fell; it rose again, and dragged on and on, with gasp, and groan, and malediction, until it came to the house temporarily occupied by the Marleys. All in front was dark. The figure went to the back. There was a light in the back sitting room, on the ground floor. The windows were nearly even with the ground, and looking in at one of them, there could be seen, through a slight opening in the large heavy curtains, which had not been fully drawn, a handsome, well-furnished room, dimly lighted by two candles. On a sofa, by the fire, lay a gentleman, evidently in the last stage of illness. The intruder gently tried the window. It was not fastened. In a moment the figure was in the room, concealed only by the curtains.

There entered the room, her hand pressed closely

to her side, a tall, stout lady, her eyes shining brilliantly, but her face deathly pale. She bent over the invalid.

"The solicitor," she murmured.

" Bring him in," was the very faint reply.

The lady went to the door, and returned with a tall, good-featured, but sinister-looking man, who crept along the carpet as though he were afraid of waking a bloodthirsty giant. He placed upon the table a short document.

" This is in accordance with the instructions I gave you this morning ?" whispered the invalid.

"Yes."

The sick man tried to read the paper.

" Ah, I'm past that," he moaned ; "read it to me, if you please."

The solicitor read the document in a low tone.

" Yes, that will do ; I will sign it," was painfully gasped.

" One moment," interposed the solicitor ; " we must have witnesses. O, mercy ! Mrs. Marley, you are all on fire !" and catching up the paper, the lawyer hastened to her assistance.

The lady sprang back, and knocked one of the candles on to the floor.

" No harm done—none in the least," she said, hurriedly, becoming as flushed as she before was pale. " There, dear [to the invalid], I'm so sorry—so very sorry—my sleeve is only a little singed, that is all. Now I will find a witness;" and she went to the door.

"I'm a witness!" said a deep voice; and Harry Marley, worn and wasted almost as his father, and clothed in rags and tatters as a poor vagrant, advanced to the table.

Mrs. Marley uttered a loud cry.

"Not too late, father—not too late! Oh! say a word, say a word! I am Harry—*your* Harry," exclaimed the young man, falling on his knees by his father's side, and clutching his hands.

Mrs. Marley recovered herself.

"Take him away, Taverly—hurl him off—he'll rob and murder us. Strike him down, I say."

Rising from his feet, the youth caught the lawyer by the throat, with all the strength he could muster.

"You villain, you atrocious scoundrel!" he hissed. "I've watched you, you false knave! give me that will you've put in your pocket. I've seen it all."

"Idiot—fool!" shrieked Mrs. Marley. "Strangle him, Charles—kill him, you blockhead! Here, if you have become a woman, I must be a man!" and seizing the candlestick which had been thrown down, she advanced, and dealt a heavy blow upon——

Not the youth—for, almost by an incredible effort, the apparently dying man on the sofa roused and threw himself between them. The blow lighted on him, and stretched him senseless.

The infuriated woman drew back, aghast and shivering. A cry arose from the son, which was heard throughout the house, and the servants rushed into the room.

"Raise your master, and cast that villain out of window!" shrieked Mrs. Marley.

"Seize her!" shouted Harry. "He is my father—she has killed him!"

The servants hung back: Mrs. Marley threw on them a withering glance, and, with a scream of rage, rushed forward to assist Taverly. The little table, on which stood the remaining candle, was knocked down. The servants ran for lights. The scuffling continued for a few seconds, and there was a heavy fall.

The end had come.

Not to the poor sufferer on the floor—for, strange to say, he recovered, and lived many years. Not to the hapless youth—for he, too, grew strong and well again, and is alive now. Not to the tricky lawyer—for, unrecognized by the respectable members of the profession, he yet practises and legally defrauds. But to the scheming, bad, heartless woman. Even when she had pondered that day upon "twenty years' more enjoyment, or five-and-twenty, or thirty—why not say thirty?" the end was surely drawing near, It had come now. The retribution had fallen.

———

The foregoing narrative can scarcely be included in the "Recollections of a Relieving Officer," seeing that Mr. Jones figures in it to only a slight extent, and that the principal circumstances were communicated to me through other sources. However, I have thought the story interesting, and therefore have strained a point and presented it.

X.—DESPERATE DEBORAH.

Mr. Jones and I were chattering about refractory paupers.

" You don't remember 'Desperate Deborah,' do you, sir ?"asked the Relieving Officer. " But you would not, though," he added. " She was before your time. A beautiful creature she was, most certainly! I never had to deal with one like her, and I sincerely trust such another may not arrive while I'm Relieving Officer."

" What's become of her ?"

" Oh, she married at last, and is now living, quite as a lady, over in Tarnsey yonder. Her poverty was brought to a close in a most singular manner."

" Let's have the story, Mr. Jones."

Well, sir, it's not a very long one. Deborah Tomkinson was the daughter of a very humble shopkeeper in Bramblestone, a widower. Who John Tomkinson was, and where he came from, nobody ever knew. He was an elderly man, very reserved and very cross. Only one man ever had the boldness to ask him for particulars of himself, and Tomkinson replied by catching the man

by the throat, and nearly strangled him. No one, after
that, put to Tomkinson any similar question. Well,
Deborah was his daughter. She was a wonder in two
ways. First, she was a perfect giantess, fully six feet
high, and broad in proportion, and her arms were like a
strong blacksmith's. Secondly, her temper was the
most violent you can imagine. The least thing sent her
into a frenzy, and she would lay about her, right and
left, in a way to demolish everything around her. She
and her father quarrelled fearfully. All the people in
the town knew and dreaded her, and she came to be
called "Desperate Deborah,"—not in her presence,
though, I should remark. I scarcely think there was a
man in the place who would so have styled her within
her hearing.

The father died; Deborah was left destitute. One
day she made her appearance at the Union Office. I
was out. Mr. Flack attended to her.

"I want relief."

"Sorry it's come to that, Deborah," replied the Assistant, mildly; "you must appear before the Board
on Thursday. Do you need anything in the mean
time?"

"Of course I do. I want bread, and meat, and beer.
Do I look as though I lived on air?"

"Can't say you do, Deborah," replied Mr. Flack.
"Well, I'll give you a half-quartern loaf, just for the
present, and when Mr. Jones——"

"Give me a half-quartern loaf!" screamed the young

lady. "What's the good of that? Come, I must have half-a-crown! Out with it!"

"Now, Deborah," urged Mr. Flack, gently, for there was no help handy, and he was but a little man, "be reasonable; take the bread, and, as I've told you, when Mr. Jones——"

"Give me the loaf," she interrupted.

"There, there's a nice one," said Mr. Flack, with a sickly smile, taking one from off a very high shelf, which he reached by a ladder, and handing it to her.

"Thank you—I am so grateful," was Deborah's reply; and, as she uttered it, with one bound she was over the counter.

"That shelf wants an ornament," cried the gentle member of the fair sex. "It shall have one;" and, in an instant, she had Mr. Flack in her arms, and had deposited him on the shelf whence he had taken the bread. And there, as she had removed the ladder, I found him, on my return in the course of a few minutes, nervously peeping over, after the manner of a very young kitten, not yet able to jump.

. But this was only the beginning. Deborah the Desperate had now declared war against the Union authorities, and she carried it on with vigour. Her mode of conducting war had this leading characteristic: "Strike the enemy at all times, and under all circumstances." She no sooner caught sight of anybody having any connection with the Union, than she made after him; and as a battle with her was not to be contemplated, if it could be avoided, the enemy invariably sought safety in flight. I remember my extreme astonishment at seeing, on the Wednesday prior to the Thursday on which she was to be examined by the guardians, a highly-respectable guardian, named Tourneville (a Frenchman), trotting along the street, gasping, groaning, and ejaculating in manner quite frightful. I tried to stop him, inquiring the cause of his perturbation.

"Go away, go away!" he shouted, vehemently. "Not stop me, dear Mr. Jones, not stop me;" and he plunged forward, like a madman.

I looked round, and saw Deborah in the distance, and —well, I don't mind owning it—I was out of the way in two seconds.

I had an appointment with Mr. Tourneville that afternoon, at the Union House. Instead of keeping it, he sent me a note, which ran thus :—

"Dear Sir,—I am quite precluded by circumstances from coming to you. Please come to me. You will find the back gate open.
                    "Truly yours,
                        "J. TOURNEVILLE."

"Very odd!" thought I, as I trudged over. "Why should I go in the back way, I wonder ?"

The moment I was in the house, its master clutched me by the arm.

"Havn't been out, not one yard, since the morning," he said, in a subdued voice.

"Not ill, I hope?" I said.

"No, not sick," he replied; "but—but—look here —see what you see."

I looked from the front window, and, not far off, I descried the terrible Deborah, evidently keeping a lynx-eye upon the house.

"Just you read," said Mr. Tourneville, and he put into my hand a dirty scrap of paper. "This was left here to-day."

I read as follows:—

"Villin!—I yer you have been torking agin *me*. When I sees you, I'll have a little parly woo with you. .
"Servant,
"DEBORAH."

The next day she was had up before the Board of Guardians. I remember there was a great discussion as to whether we should not forego seeing her; but we were ashamed of the laugh which would arise, if, in her case, we deviated from our rule.

"Here we are, twelve men," observed the Chairman, "and there's the porter outside. Surely we can manage one woman."

So Miss Deborah was ushered in. I know we all quaked at the sight of her. She seemed in excellent health, and had she been of the other sex, her vast dimensions would have excited extreme admiration. She gazed at us defiantly. Mr. Potts, who was sitting close to where she stood, remembered some instructions which he ought to have given to his servant, and left us.

"Well, Deborah," cried the Chairman, good-humouredly, "what can we do for you?"

"What's the good of that sort of talk?" was the disdainful counter-question. "You know what I want, well enough. Mind ye make no game of me now; I ain't at all in a mind to bear it." And she looked at us much as a giant might look upon a saucy schoolboy who was nettling him.

"There, now, don't be angry, Deborah," said the Chairman.

"Then you please to talk reasonable," replied the damsel, with dignity. "I'm as a quiet as a lamb, except I'm aggravated."

"Just so, Deborah. Well, now, I think if we give you two-and-sixpence a-week, you'll be able to get on."

"Not enough."

"Well, but, Deborah, we have heavy claims upon us; you'll earn something, you know."

"No work. Say three-and-sixpence."

Now, "Desperate Deborah" had behaved very well to this point, and, if left to be dealt with exclusively by the Chairman, would have been satisfactorily disposed of; but, unluckily, there sat in the corner, at the furthest distance of anybody from our excitable customer, a guardian of the name of Rubbles, a touchy, testy man, who must needs chime in as follows :—

"My good woman, you know you can either take the

half-crown or leave it, just as you like. We can't stop here all day discussing the point with you."

The Chairman groaned audibly. "It's all up," he whispered to me. "We're in for it."

And so we were. I saw Deborah's eyes glisten. The guardians shuffled uneasily in their seats.

"And who are you, pray?" screamed the playful maiden, her arms working, her fingers twirling, and her head nodding in a manner truly ominous.

. "Now, Deborah," interposed the Chairman.

"Oh, yes; it's 'now Deborah,' indeed. Better call me 'Desperate Deborah' at once. Ah! I know what you call me. And as for that skinflint in the corner there, out of this room I'll not go, until I've let him see what Deborah can do. So here goes."

"Upon my word, sir," continued Mr. Jones, "it's no figure of speech to say that the scene which ensued beggared all description. The amiable young lady made first a furious plunge to reach Mr. Rubbles; and it would have served him right, for his thoughtlessness, to have surrendered him to her. But we, nevertheless, interposed, and a general fight ensued. And for a minute or so the twelve men actually got the worst of it. For, you see, the frenzied woman pummelled into us with her fists, while we, although writhing under her blows, forbore doing more than endeavouring to restrain her. The yells from the unfortunate dozen of men who were thus being ruthlessly pounded were absolutely dreadful. Somehow or other, Deborah's bare arms

K

always slipped from our hold, and then the released members inflicted blows upon her nearest foes, which would have delighted the heart of a prize-fighter. At length, the porter, who had come to our aid, ungallantly grasped the enemy's legs, and Deborah descended to the floor with a force which shook the building. But to keep her prostrate was no small difficulty, and, in despair, we were ultimately obliged, until further assistance arrived to—I am almost ashamed to say——".

"Sit upon her, I suppose, Mr. Jones?".

"Well, that was actually the case. There was no other mode of doing it."

"And what was done with her afterwards?"

"Oh! we had her up before the magistrates, and she had ten days' imprisonment, with hard labour. Her time ended, she came out as brisk as ever, and was taken into the workhouse. There, one day, she found her way to the master's apartments, captured his good lady, whom she discovered alone, carried her to a coalcellar, and locked her up; and to release her, such a contest ensued, that it really appeared as though a life or two would be lost. At length, however, Deborah found her master, and, strange to say, she did so in a little man, whom you would have thought she could crush with a hug.

"There lived at that time, in Bramblestone, a young carpenter, named Spivil. He used to be called Lucky Frank, from the circumstance that, though not particularly clever, industrious, or persevering, he jogged on

in the world much more comfortably than his fellows.
Good things, that he never expected, seemed always to
be falling to 'Lucky Frank.' This enviable person was
one day standing talking to me at the Union counter,
when Deborah, who had been discharged from the house
a few days previously, walked in. She was evidently
in a mischievous mood, and the first thing she did was,
as Frank was a little in her way, to take off his cap
and fling it into the street. Frank said not a word, but
fetched his cap, and on his return he bestowed a slap on
Deborah's bonnet, which entirely altered its fashion,
without trouble to the bonnet-maker. The result was a
furious battle. I need not trouble you, sir, with the
elevating details. I didn't interfere, and in a few
minutes the contest ended in Deborah being stretched
on the ground. It was a marvellous victory for Frank.
His usual fortune, of course, came to his aid, and instead of being reduced to a jelly, as might have been
expected, he stood a victor. Deborah got up quietly
and walked away.

"It might have been ten days after this when the
news reached me that Frank and Deborah were going
to be married. I was utterly astounded. I couldn't
help seeing Frank, and remonstrating with him. He
—'Lucky Frank!'—to be entering into such a preposterous alliance!

"'But why not?' he asked, calmly.

"'Mercy on me!' I exclaimed. 'You must be mad
even to think of it.'

" ' There's nothing against her but her temper, and she is such a wonderfully fine woman ! Yet, you know, I mastered her.'

" Here was the secret. The giantess was an object of unqualified admiration to little Frank ; and then the having conquered her in the struggle had so delighted him, he was always thinking of her, and at length came to feel an odd sort of affection for her.

" ' But is she willing to have you ?' I asked.

" ' She doats upon me,' answered the lover. ' She told me that the very moment I had her on the ground, she felt I was the man for her, and she could do any-thing for me.'

" ' Well,' I said, inwardly marvelling at this new instance of the strange workings of Cupid, ' I hope and trust the next person wanted after the priest won't be the coroner.' And with this ungracious remark, I left him.

" They were married. The whole neighbourhood deemed Frank a lunatic, but he had his way. I am bound to admit the truth, there was nothing against Deborah but her temper ; and after the marriage I was told she had much improved, and that she and her hus-band agreed admirably.

" One afternoon, at the expiration of a month, I was informed a gentleman, a solicitor from London, wished to speak to me. He came in.

" ' Have you a young woman in your workhouse named Deborah Tomkinson ?' he asked.

"'We had, a short time ago,' I replied. 'Her name is now Spivil. She is married to a carpenter, whose shop is at the end of the next street, on the left.'

"'Oh! very well; that's all right. Bless my heart! what a deal of trouble I have had over this affair.'

"'May I ask its nature?'

"'Yes; it's no secret. This young woman, I take it, from information I've received, is the only daughter of a man named John Tomkinson, who lived here.'

"'Just so.'

"'Well, that Tomkinson was brother to a deceased client of mine—James Tomkinson, of London. It seems the brothers quarrelled in early life, and all communication ceased between them. My client, an old bachelor, is recently dead, and in his will he leaves to his brother, or child, or children, all he died possessed of, value, say five thousand pounds. I thought for a while that the whole would go to the Crown; but, luckily, I stumbled on a clue to John Tomkinson's movements, ascertained the place of his death, and here I am.'"

"Lucky Frank, sir!" said Mr. Jones, in conclusion, "I believe he has really an excellent wife, and every source of quiet happiness. You should hear the good-natured, kind-hearted Mrs. Spivil laugh over the recollections of 'Desperate Deborah!'"

XI.—RETRIBUTION.

MR. JONES and I were passing Bramblestone church-yard. A gentleman and lady, both mild and pleasant looking, stood silently contemplating one of the graves.

"Mr. and Mrs. Daunt," whispered the Relieving Officer.

I nodded.

Everybody about Bramblestone knew that upright, loving couple.

PART I.

MOVED by a soft strain of music, a man will some-times turn his face upward, and look as though a para-dise were opening above him. Opposite a striking pic-ture a beholder will become as a statue. But a man, standing with his back to a wall, feasting his eyes upon a workhouse, is, indeed, an odd sight. Thus, however, a man stood, and thus was he engaged one evening, many years ago.

It was Bramblestone Workhouse which was so singu-larly an object of pleasant contemplation. The New Poor Law had not then been enacted, and Mr. Jones, subsequently Relieving Officer, was quite a young man, and had just been appointed Overseer. He was coming, on the night in question, to visit the "House," when the person first mentioned addressed him.

"Well, Mr. Jones, making your usual visit? Going

to see John Daunt among the rest of the poor devils, eh? He was always demented—now he's uncommonly Daunted, I take it. Ha! ha!"

The tone of Mr. Jones's reply was civil, and nothing beyond.

"Yes sir; my customary visit, as you say. You are almost as regular as I am."

"True; I like to come and look at the horrid, dreary walls. There's something in the sight of those slips of windows, which pleases me. Old Jericho! why it's like a furnace out here, to-night. What must it be in rooms with such windows as those? But, tell me, how is Daunt? Dying by this time, I should think!"

Mr. Jones's shrug of disgust was not observable in the partial darkness.

"Yes he's dying, Mr. Mayner. But excuse me. Good night. I'm behind time." And he hurried away.

Mr. Mayner knocked the ashes from his cigar, replaced it in his mouth, and sauntered away likewise.

To be effeminate—to be weak in feeling and resolve —one shrinks from that notion, as picturing something so poor and mean. But to be bold and strong, and to be moved by the spirit of a fiend, is awful. John Daunt was a humble, shrinking creature from his boyhood; and, from his boyhood, Ralph Mayner was an unscrupulous, determined villain. How these two men came to love the same woman is a mystery; but only one could have her. Ellen Leslie became the wife of John Daunt.

For Daunt actually ran away with her. If for one single instant, in the course of this dark story, I can allow myself to smile, it must be at the thought of this enterprise on the part of such a man as Daunt. But he was urged to it by despair. He knew that Ellen's parents were well-nigh forcing her into a marriage with his rival. He knew that rival's character well. There was no time to be lost. The pair went away by moonlight, and were married. A year afterwards, Ellen Daunt gave birth to a son, and died.

As time rolled on, additional troubles fell upon Daunt. A fatality seemed to hang over all he undertook. He had settled near Bramblestone as a small farmer. For some years he just managed to live; but an unseen influence was perpetually dodging around him, damaging his character and credit, indisposing people to deal with him, and causing him loss in various ways. Though he knew it not, Ralph Mayner was busy. When that monster heard of the elopement, he said with a great oath, "I'll never leave him, till I've crushed him." And, bringing his acute intellect and unswerving will to bear, backed by means and influence, which he possessed to some extent, he so environed John Daunt with nets and pitfalls, that, although it was a work of years, it was a work done most effectually at last. John Daunt, one night, took his boy's hand, saying, "God help us, Sydney! Your father is penniless and friendless!"

Aye; there was not a single person who came forward with the smallest aid. A brief struggle, and then poor

John and his boy were actually received into Bramble-stone Workhouse.

Ralph Mayner heard the news. He had married some years before, and had one child,—a daughter. He was now a widower.

It was a very hot summer. Mayner came, with his little girl, to Bramblestone, and took apartments outside the town, where, as I have already acquainted the reader, the views were pretty and the air salubrious. Mayner then made acquaintance with the workhouse officials, learned all particulars in regard to Daunt, and did not hesitate to avow his hatred against him, although he did not communicate the cause.

Dead!—there was the end. John Daunt died very shortly after his admission into the workhouse. Ralph Mayner had fulfilled his oath; he had crushed his rival; his power was ended now.

But he would see the funeral.

One fine, warm morning, they laid poor John Daunt in his grave, in Bramblestone churchyard. One mourner followed him,—his boy, Sydney, who was about twelve years of age. Yet, may be, more sorrow attended the funeral than has oftentimes been present when scores of sombre faces have formed a dismal group round the graveside. The ceremony over, the officials departed, leaving the weeping boy to follow when he pleased.

There had been gazing at the spectacle throughout, the hard-hearted Ralph Mayner and his pretty, pecu-

liar-featured, gentle-looking daughter, some six years
old. I fancy even Ralph experienced an unusual emotion, when the ceremony was over. He must have felt
that now, indeed, the tragedy of "John Daunt and his
Foe" was fully played out. At all events his eyelids
drooped, and he let go his child's hand. On being released, the little girl trotted away to Sydney Daunt,
who was just leaving.

"Poor boy!" she said, gently, giving him a sixpence.
"Don't cry."

He motioned her away, and would not take the
money.

"Do take it," urged the tiny maiden; "I have plenty." (Children always fancy you refuse their gifts
from a notion they are robbing themselves.)

The boy gazed at her in surprise. He didn't manifest any touching emotion, dear friend reader. If he had
been of the class perpetually turning up in certain novels,
he would have burst into tears anew, have uplifted his
hands, and exclaimed, "Now, may heaven's bright light
be ever reflected from your sweet face, young lady!" or
something equally poetical; but being only a poor
workhouse boy, like thousands besides, he simply felt
and looked uncouth and shy. But the scene was soon
ended. Waking from his reverie, Ralph Mayner witnessed, with extreme surprise and anger, the communication passing between the children. He ran to the spot,
caught his little girl roughly with one hand, and with the
other, seized Sydney's cap, and flung it over the church-

yard wall. Now, for several minutes past, there had
been leaning over that wall, watching the parties, a
respectably-attired, hearty, healthy-faced man, on the
unfavourable side of sixty. I may as well say, at once,
that this person was a London tradesman, who had been
staying in Bramblestone a fortnight, and was returning
the next day. He was an eccentric being, had not a
relative in the world; but, as compensation, had plenty
of money. Sydney's cap had not touched the ground
before he was by Mayner's side, shaking in his face a
robust fist, that made Ralph shrink back.

" You're a brute, and a beast, and a vile scaramouch,"
cried the indignant tradesman. "If I had my will,
you should break stones all day, and sleep on thistles all
night," he added; and then, turning his back on the astonished Mayner, the curious old gentleman seized Sydney by the hand, hurried him out of the churchyard,
and then bade him "tell him all about it."

Thus enjoined, the boy communicated the entire history of his woes, and those of his deceased father.

"Would you come with me to London?" inquired his
newly-found friend, when he had done.

" Gladly," was the answer.

Without further discussion the two went to the workhouse. Application was made for leave to remove the
boy, which, after the usual forms, was granted; and
very quickly the tradesman and his charge were on
their way to London. It was a long, long while before
Bramblestone again heard of Sydney Daunt.

PART II.

TWENTY years. In that period round changes, both
for good and for evil, come to pass. Twenty years from
the ending of the first part of this story had brought
grey hairs to Ralph Mayner, and with them anxieties
and troubles which bore hard upon him. He had
speculated, and been unsuccessful; and now, with
broken health and soured temper, he found himself with
a cloud of difficulties hanging over him. He was not a
poor man even now, but he had become involved in a
variety of schemes, so intertwined, that unless he could
keep them all healthily afloat, the whole would collapse
and ruin him. That gloomy issue stared him awkwardly in the face at this very time. A period of
general and great pressure had arisen. Everybody was
trying to borrow—nobody seemed willing to lend.
Ralph wanted a couple of thousand pounds. Wanted
it!—he must have it. It was a life and death matter
to him—he would be ruined without it. In a few days,
acceptances to that amount would come due. If they
were dishonoured, Ralph would be utterly prostrated.

And yet he had tried in every quarter, and failed
Ralph frightened his kind, loving daughter, Annie—he
looked at times so stern, and became so fickle in his
humour.

They sat together one evening.

"I am going to London to-morrow," said Ralph,
abruptly.

" To-morrow, papa, and so unwell as you are !"

"Yes, Annie; you know I'm on the brink of ruin."

" O my dear father !"

" There, pray don't cry. I hate crying. People should never cry after they are six years old. But I want you to know exactly how the case stands. Bills for two thousand pounds will come due in the course of a day or two. They must be taken up, or we must go out of the country. I have no money available, and no one will lend me any. The only chance left is in seeing Cawsher, the solicitor. He has refused by letter; but I think, if I could see him, he would alter his mind."

" But, dear papa, even should he refuse, surely we need not leave England. If the people who hold these securities will only give you time you will pay them."

Ralph laughed grimly.

" Perhaps they might, under ordinary circumstances, Annie; but there is one small unfortunate feature about these bills which will interfere. Can you guess it?"

"Not in the least, papa."

" I forged them, Annie."

A little scream, and a deadly faintness, were the results of this communication.

" There, now, Annie, don't let us have heroics, or hysterics, or anything of the kind. Listen ! There is no reason why you should deem your father worse than he really is. If ever there was a palliation for—for the act I have mentioned, it is here. The people owed me the money, and would neither pay me nor give me their acceptances. I was shockingly pressed, and at length I made the bills. If I can find the money to what is called ' retire' them, in a couple of days, all will be well. If I cannot, I must run away. If they catch me, they will transport me for life."

Ralph said all this in a jaunty way, with his back to the fire, and his arms under his coat tails. Annie sat pale and shivering.

"So, Annie, the first thing in the morning, you'll pack up as much as you can without creating wonderment in the house, and we'll go together to London. Now, my candle, please, and we'll to bed. Kiss me, Annie. Bless my heart, the silly thing's all in a quiver, and her lips and cheek are as cold as ice. You must get over these school-girl shakings, Annie. Your father never remembers being a boy. At your age you should be no longer as a child."

To London they went. They found apartments in a not very lively locality—Salisbury Street, in the Strand. To Crawsher, the solicitor, straightway repaired Mr. Mayner.

"Ah, Mr. Mayner, how d'ye do?" cried Crawsher, buoyantly, extending his hand. "Staying in town, eh?"

"For a very short time," replied Ralph. "Some trifling matters want attending to. I wrote you the other day."

"Yes, and I replied. I should have been delighted, you know; but, bless me, just at this moment, we, in London, are all on the brink of ruin," and Crawsher rubbed his hands slowly, and his face was radiant with smiles.

"Well, the case is this," said Ralph; "I should be very glad of that money, if you can in any way manage it. No great consequence, of course; but still, just at this time——".

"My dear sir," interrupted the lawyer; "there really is no money. I don't think I could squeeze out a fifty-pound note to save my own father from bankruptcy."

"Humph!" grunted Ralph, "it will bother me."

Crawsher's only reply was to put his hands in his pockets, and look more benevolent than before.

"How's Miss Annie?" he asked, after a pause.

"Oh, middling," replied Ralph.

An expression crept across his face, which Crawsher did not observe.

"By the way, when did you see young Lucerne last?" he inquired.

"Six weeks back."

"Then you don't know what's occurred?"

"Eh? No. Nothing bad, I hope, to Lucerne; for he's a nice young fellow—plenty of money, and a good client."

"He's about making somebody a good husband," said Ralph, significantly.

"What!" cried Crawsher. "You don't mean—is it—Is he going to marry our dear young lady?"

Ralph nodded. (A great vagabond was Ralph.)

"I'm astounded! All settled?"

"Everything."

"Humph! I'm right glad. A little business for me, too. I shall have Lucerne here shortly, no doubt, about the settlement. Ha! ha! But, stay, I'm forgetting your own particular matter."

"Oh if there's not fifty pounds to be had——" Ralph was beginning cavalierly.

"Oh, well, never mind that; we must see, you know. I've a client, the *protégé* of an old tradesman, who has lately died and left him a heap of money. He'll want to see you himself, for he's rather a funny customer. But come here the first thing in the morning, and I daresay we shall manage it. Good-bye! Good-bye!"

"I think we shall be able to go back to Bramblestone safe and sound, Annie," said Ralph, when he had returned to his daughter.

"Thank God, papa!"

"There's no doubt he'll do it, I think," muttered Ralph to himself. "It's running it rather close, though. I must have the money to-morrow."

Early the next morning Ralph was with Crawsher.

"Well," said the latter, "my man is in the other room."

"Can I have the money at once?" asked Ralph, with barely concealed anxiety.

"He'll give you the cheque in this room, my friend. I know he'll do it, for he said so; but he want's to see you."

He walked to the door of an inner room, and opened it.

"Walk in, Mr. Daunt. Will you be kind enough ?

Mr. Daunt, Mr. Mayner. Mr. Mayner——Eh! Bless
me! what's wrong?"

Nothing, so far as Sydney Daunt was concerned, for
the lawyer's communication had revealed to him (though
he had said nothing to the lawyer) to whom he was
asked to lend; but Ralph fell back, saying, huskily—

"Have we seen each other before, sir?"

"I am Sydney Daunt," was the reply. "Twenty
years since, you and I were in Bramblestone churchyard.
Nay, don't turn away, Mr. Mayner; let that sad story
drop; I have no desire for what men call revenge.
You want a couple of thousand pounds—there is the
cheque."

But even in that dire extremity, Ralph Mayner was
Ralph Mayner—the watcher of Bramblestone workhouse; the cruel witness in Bramblestone churchyard;
his features quivering, his limbs shaking in spite of him,
so that he had to grasp the table for support.

"And do you think," he uttered, in a hoarse voice,
"that I am become a weak, cry-baby thing like John
Daunt, your father? Oh, this is beautiful! Here is a
scene! Here is Christian vengeance! Shall I go upon
my knees, and weep over you, young man? Shall I
beg a blessing on you, and entreat forgiveness for the
past? Hark ye, now! I would be torn limb from
limb first! Sooner than take that cheque, I'd burn
myself bit by bit in yonder fire. I hate you! You
have your triumph, you white-faced school girl; but it
shall go no further. Even now, Ralph Mayner can

L

despise you from the bottom of his soul, and can hurl at you a lasting defiance."

And he rushed from the room into the street, mad and desperate.

Many hours had passed, and Annie had become uneasy on account of her father's lengthened absence. Towards afternoon she determined to seek him at Mr. Crawshor's office, which she knew to be in Gray's Inn. Being quite unacquainted with London, it is not strange that she lost her way, and, on inquiry, found herself much fatigued near Hyde Park. She was standing, looking woefully about her, when a gentleman passed, gazed at her intently, and then stopped.

"I fancy I speak to Miss Annie Mayner," he said, still scanning her.

She bowed, hesitatingly.

"Do you remember Sydney Daunt, to whom you offered sixpence, very many years back, in Bramblestone churchyard? It is a circumstance *I* have never forgotten."

She recollected the occurrence well, she said.

"You are Mr. Daunt," she added quickly with emotion, for painful recollections were awakened at the name.

"Yes. Might he ask—she seemed fatigued—whether he could be of any service to her?"

She told him her trouble.

"Your father left Gray's Inn, as I happen to know, several hours back."

"If he might detain her ten minutes, and she would walk in the park with him, he should much like to say a few words."

She consented, and Sydney related briefly what had occurred in the morning. When he had concluded, he said,—

"Even now, I have but one feeling, and that is to help him in his difficulty."

"You don't know how great his difficulty is," thought Annie.

"Will you let me accompany you to your apartments? I will again assure you of my desire towards him."

Annie agreed. Knowing what she did, and hearing what she did now, she was greatly alarmed on her father's account. They proceeded in a cab to Salisbury Street.

The driver pulled up some doors before they reached the number given him.

"Quick! quick!" cried Sydney, out of the window.

"Can't go no further, sir," was the answer. "Blocked up. There's a mob round the door you want to go in at."

A thrill passed through both Sydney and Annie.

The cabman made inquiry of a bystander.

"It's a man as lodges in that house as has been and drowned hisself," continued the cabman; "they're takin' on him in now."

In a moment the cab was empty, and a man, bearing a shrieking girl in his arms, was speeding through the mob.

Ralph Mayner and John Daunt lie near together in Bramblestone churchyard. Thither go Sydney and Annie Daunt (the loving husband and wife), and gaze upon their graves :—

" God's judgments are a great deep."

XII.—THE ELECTION OF A MEDICAL OFFICER.

Amongst Mr. Jones's stories was the following. Agreeably to the pledge referred to in it, it was not related until after the death of the principal personage.

Many years back, Bramblestone, although a large place, contained only three medical practitioners, and even these had not much to do, for the Bramblestonians enjoyed good health, and lived long. One of the doctors was himself a marvel. Old Mr. Stephenson, at eighty-six was still full of vigour. He was the Workhouse Medical Officer, (the Union had just been formed) and he doctored the inmates, when sick, with very peculiar medicine indeed, such, as I suppose, no Medical Officer ever supplied before, or ever will again. Heaps of delicacies, and the good things of this life, all prepared by the Doctor's housekeeper, who was about his own age, and who, in the blessed work of their preparation, knew a happiness of which very few titled dames have even a conception.

A dark day came to Bramblestone. The dear old man was sick, even unto death. Doctors do not prescribe for themselves. I am not aware why. Perhaps knowing how much mischief they have, in their time, inflicted upon others, they shrink from the idea of experimenting on their own bodies. It is just possible that the knowledge which Smith is quite sure, from experience, is not in himself, may be in Brown; so brother disciple of the healing art is called in, and is afforded an opportunity of ridding himself of a rival. To attend Mr. Stephenson, Mr. Endemwell was hastily summoned. He looked at his aged fellow-labourer, and thought probably he had had work enough. The poor old Doctor lay motionless. "What had he taken?"

"He had done pretty well, sir," moaned the afflicted housekeeper, "up to last night; but since then he's had a mere nothing."

"What do you mean by 'a mere nothing?'" testily inquired Mr. Endemwell.

"He's had a mite of roast beef and pickles, with the tiniest bit of custard pudding, a morsel of cheese, and scarcely half a glass of ale; but he couldn't even look at the beautiful beef tea I made for him," replied the old lady, bursting into an uncontrollable fit of weeping.

Now Mr. Endemwell had but about a hundred and fifty pounds a year upon which to support himself, a wife, and a family of six children, including an idiot, poor fellow, whose deficiency of intellect seemed provocative of a never ending appetite, for he ate as much as three of the other children. Under these circumstances, Mr. Endemwell occasionally took "a mere nothing" from a different cause to that which was operating on his aged patient.

"Killing himself!" exclaimed Mr. Endemwell, uplifting his palms. "Vigorous measures, Mrs. Trim, vigorous measures must be resorted to."

And so they were. That malicious monster went home, and at once retired to his study. After half-an-hour he came out again, looking like a man determined to do his duty at every cost. And he went into his surgery, and taking a phial, he filled it with equal proportions of four most villainous-complexioned liquids. Then he made up four pills, and concluded by preparing a blister of dimensions which so frightened the shop-boy, who happened to come in as the work was done, that he turned very sick, and was obliged to be dosed on the spot. Finally, when the boy was better, the dreadful package was despatched to Mr. Stephenson, with particular instructions.

The poor old gentleman was buried amid the sobs of the Bramblestonians, (I have thought it unnecessary, looking at the foregoing, to tell you that he died very quickly indeed) and Bramblestone had now but two Doctors.

One of these, of course, was Mr. Endemwell, and the other Mr. Johnston. The latter was a young man,

and had not been long in Bramblestone. Nevertheless
he was much liked, and had a good practice, partly
through his undoubted ability, and partly through the
support which had been afforded to him by the late Mr.
Stephenson.

Directly the decease of their representative in Parlia-
ment is announced to a constituency, the electors at the
same moment express concern at the event and wonderment
as to who shall succeed to the vacant place. Within an hour
after Mr. Stephenson's departure, strife was busy in
Bramblestone, hostile feelings raged strongly, old friends
had quarrelled, new alliances had been formed, plots and
counterplots, whisperings, questionings, debatings, praise
and abuse, agitation, hope, doubt, fear—such as had not
had play in Bramblestone for some time, rose up and
flourished in a manner that was quite startling. Who
was to be the new Medical Officer to the Workhouse ?
Mr. Endemwell's friends claimed the berth for him almost as a matter of common honesty. That indefatig-
able practitioner had helped to place so many Bramblestonians in their last homes, that it was the merest gratitude to give him any good thing that might fall in the way.

The Workhouse was very full, too, at the time, and a
clever, expeditious medical attendant like Mr. Endemwell might be enabled, indirectly, to effect a reduction
in the forthcoming poor rate. Certain it was that Mr.
Endemwell was immediately put forward as a candidate
for the vacant office, and mollified at the poor doctor's
new prospects, it is equally certain that his landlord put

back or delayed an execution for rent which he had long threatened, and had been about levying.

But then there immediately came such a shock to the Endemwells. All of a sudden, Mr. Johnstone announced that he should stand. Here was presumption! Here was a monstrous invasion of the proper order of things! Who would support this audacious young man? Alas! it soon appeared he would not want supporters. Actually the Chairman of the Union would propose him, and it was said Lord Lorgbow was in his favour. When Mr. Endemwell heard this last intelligence, he fell into a state of mind which had well nigh caused the death of half his patients: for he was making up the medicines at the time, and in his rage and anguish, thinking of nothing but slaughter and destruction, he put into each potion a comfortable little dose of arsenic, and had he not fortunately recovered his senses before the medicines were sent out, and recollected his performance, there would indeed have been weeping in every house in Bramblestone, save one, perhaps, the undertaker's. "Business is business," and had that respected functionary consoled himself with the old adage of " It's an ill wind &c.," we must have forgiven him.

Presently great placards appeared,—" Endemwell for Medical Officer," and underneath were smaller announcements (serving as a kind of Testimonial) of a new work by the learned practitioner, entitled, "Endemwell on the consequences of Excess of Eating and Drinking "— although, by the by, it was scarcely likely that this

peculiar class of disorders would often come under his
treatment in the Workhouse.   If Mrs. Endemwell had
had her way, she could have put forth a much more
pointed and stirring appeal to the Guardians of Bramblestone.   She would not have minded drawing attention in
some delicate but touching way to the painful fact of the
six children and the idiot's appetite.   She shocked the
poor doctor by telling him so openly.   The landlord's
threats, and the butcher's and baker's remonstrances,
had eased the struggling wife of all her pride.   Why
should not the doctor circulate something of this kind?
"Endemwell for Medical Officer—Fathers and Mothers
of Families, remember Endemwell with a wife and six
children, one of them being an idiot, with a large appetite."

"It's all very well for you to say ' Pish !' petulantly
exclaimed the troubled mother; BUT ISN'T IT THE
FACT ?"

"Of course it is, Sarah ; but your notion's outra-
geous."

"Who's to pay the bills?" cried Mrs. Endemwell,
well knowing that inquiry would tell upon the Doctor
like a tap with a sledge hammer.

"They can't be paid, that's all," moaned poor Endemwell.   "But I don't let Guardians have a moment's
peace ; sure, man never made such praiseworthy efforts
to attain an object as I've done." .

That was true.   The Guardians were well nigh out
of their senses.   Endemwell seemed ubiquitous.   But

still the battle scarcely appeared to be turning favourably to him. One man, however, advocated his cause with an energy perfectly unsurpassable. He was a little man whose wife Endemwell had attended for some trifling ailment, which under his constant care quickly and permanently ceased—the whole story is on her tombstone—this man loved Endemwell as a brother. Strange to say, he did not employ him as his own medical attendant; but no matter, he vowed he was the very man for Medical Officer to the Workhouse, and he worked for him day and night.

It was difficult to choose between the rivals, and the contest did no end of mischief in Bramblestone. The muffin and crumpet maker and his wife quarrelled over it; were high and mighty with each other, and separated. The butcher and his wife had a very warm difference indeed, insomuch that they fought; then they grew calm and came together again, and I hold them to have been much more sensible people than their lofty neighbours just mentioned. Bramblestone was quite sick of the subject, and right glad was everybody when the day of election arrived to end the worry.

It was an exciting day; the issue was very doubtful. Mr. Johnston had done his best. The Chairman had openly declared for him; Lord Longbow had half done the same. Then Lady Longbow, having had her feelings roused by a moving appeal from Mrs. Endemwell (Johnston had no wife to be his advocate), constrained his lordship to give the other half declaration in favour of Endemwell, so that his lordship's vote hung aggravatingly in the balance. The Guardians attended, every man of them. Dear to a Guardian is that privilege of electing officers. On that day the tradesmen of Bramblestone had the exquisite delight of seeing the professional men at their feet. The two candidates waited humbly in the Union Office as the Guardians passed through to the Board Room. For this occasion low bows from the professional gentlemen were only responded to by familiar and patronising nods from the tradesmen. Even when the crumpet maker awkwardly trod on Endemwell's corns, it was only one-half of the doctor's face which looked mortal enmity, the other half was all smiles and expressive gratitude.

The voting began. Endemwell's friend, the widower, rushed out to inform him that out of six votes recorded, four were in his favour, and the two were shaking hands and rejoicing when five more Guardians came in, and polled every one of them for Johnston, whereupon out came, breathless, a friend of Johnston, and fairly hugged him, assuring him that the election was virtually over, and that he was the victor. Then a noise was heard in the passage, and on Mr. Flack going out he found Mrs. Endemwell and the whole six children blocking up the passage, the idiot engaged in devouring a huge hunk of bread and butter, as though he had been just on the point of starving. Upon this Mr. Endemwell became very angry, and Mr. Johnston laughed outright, and, after a vain effort to appear dignified, poor Mrs. Endemwell fell into violent hysterics; the uproar altogether rising to a point that was quite dreadful.

All the Guardians had now attended, so the candidates knew that the poll must have closed. Mr. Endemwell asked for a glass of water, and clung to the desk-rail for support. Mr. Johnston hummed a tune and tried to look unconcerned, in which effort it is just possible he might have been successful had not his pale face, and restless eyes, and twitching limbs obstinately opposed his wishes.

The last news had been that the votes were exactly equal, since which a Guardian of doubtful disposition had passed through, and upon this man's vote the election must have turned. The Board-room door opened and the butcher came forth. He looked terribly black and fierce. As he passed Endemwell, who eyed him with secret misgiving, he bent his head, and hissed in the poor doctor's ear—

"I tell you what it is, Mr. Endemwell, if that account of mine is not settled by to-morrow night my lawyer will look you up sharp, so now you know, and don't say afterwards you didn't."

While the dismayed apothecary was staring aghast at this ominous speech, the Board-Room door opened, and the Union messenger presented himself, shouting, "Mr. Johnston will please step in."

Endemwell divined the state of things in a moment. Johnston was victorious, and was now called in to be informed of his election. The poor father of six children, including an idiot, rushed from the office, and into the street, followed by his wife and children.

It was the case. Johnston had gained the day by that last Guardian's vote. The Chairman congratulated the young man warmly, and even the Guardians who had voted against him concealed their mortification and tried to look pleased. The speech·making over, Johnston retired, and the routine business commenced. Scarcely two minutes, however, had elapsed before, to the astonishment of the Board, the young doctor reappeared in a state of great excitement, holding an open letter in his hand.

"I really do beg pardon. On my honour I beg pardon," he gasped, "but here is something I must communicate at once to the Board. Just as I was leav·ing here, a letter which had come by post to my residence was brought to me by my boy. It is from the executors of my old bachelor uncle Northop, who lived at the Land's End. The poor old man is gone at last, and has left me all his property (some twenty thousand pounds, I know, at least), upon condition that for the next five years I occupy the house in which he lived, for the purpose of completing satisfactorily certain undertakings in the neighbourhood in which he took great interest. You see, gentlemen, I've run in instantly, because my first thought has been that I could not, of course, hold the office to which you have just kindly appointed me."

That was true, so after abundant congratulations had been heaped on the fortunate Johnston, the question arose as to another election for medical officer.

"Oh, don't let's have the worry over again," said the Chairman. "Endemwell, of course, is the man. Let's appoint him at once."

And so they did; and Mr. Jones, the Relieving Officer, asked permission to run and fetch Endemwell to hear of his changed fortune.

"By all means; you're a good-hearted fellow, Jones," replied the Chairman. "Endemwell stands in want of the berth, we know. I was sorry to vote against him. Bring him here quickly, and we'll congratulate him."

Away went the Relieving Officer. Endemwell's place was not far off.

"I want Mr. Endemwell," cried Mr. Jones, hastening into the sitting-room, and accosting Mrs. Endemwell without ceremony.

"Hush, hush!" whispered the poor lady, her features so swollen as to be hardly recognisable.

The Relieving Officer drew back. "Anything wrong?" he inquired anxiously.

"He's gone in there to have a nap," was the murmured reply.

"Into the surgery to sleep?" asked Mr. Jones, in wonderment.

"I was on no account to disturb him," said Mrs. Endemwell in a lazy way, as though her wits were wandering. The Relieving Officer looked at her steadily for a moment, and seemed troubled.

"Do you know whether Mr. Endemwell has actually gone to sleep?" he asked.

"I don't hear him moving," was the listless reply.

Mr. Jonès looked through the key-hole and then tried the door. It was fastened.

"Mr. Endemwell," he cried, "it is I, Mr. Jones, Mr. Endemwell. Something important," and he knocked loudly.

"O pray, pray don't," interposed Mrs. Endemwell. "He so particularly said he was not to be roused. He will be so angry."

The Relieving Officer stooped down, and looked again through the keyhole.

"No fear of rousing him," he muttered, with much agitation, and he dashed the whole weight of his powerful frame against the door, which was literally shattered to atoms.

But notwithstanding the great noise, and the screams and cries of the alarmed wife, a figure which Mr. Jones had, through the keyhole, seen sitting calmly in the old arm-chair, sat there still, motionless.

"The Lord forgive him!" exclaimed Mr. Jones.

"Dead!" shrieked the poor wife.

Mr. Jones held up a little cup. It was sufficient answer. But even as he did so, a faint sign of life about the face attracted his attention. He grasped Mrs. Endemwell's arm.

"Now, for mercy's sake," he said, "be calm; bolt that door, and do as I say. He's not dead, we may, perhaps, save him."

Mrs. Endemwell was quiet and obedient directly.

The Relieving Officer well knew some simple but most efficacious remedy in cases of poisoning. They were vigorously applied, and in a short time Endemwell was snatched, literally, from the jaws of death. When he had somewhat recovered, Mr. Jones ran back to the Union-office, and told the Guardians that Mr. Endem-well was too poorly to attend, but would be present at their next meeting. As quickly afterwards as he could, the Relieving Officer returned to the surgery. He found Endemwell much restored, and he almost completed his restoration by telling him the circumstances connected with the appointment.

Endemwell pressed his hand warmly. "A great service, Jones, will you do it me? But I am sure you will. No one but you and my wife is aware of that," and he pointed to the surgery; "don't speak of it dur-ing my life-time. I could not bear to hear of it. I was mad then, it would drive me mad again. Will you promise me?"

The promise was readily given, and not a word was said of the circumstances until some years after Endem-well had found his home in the church-yard, and after his wife and family, who, through Endemwell's having for a long time rejoiced in a greatly increased practice, were left very tolerably provided for, had left Bramble-stone for a distant locality.

XIII.—THE MIDNIGHT AFFRAY.

A MAN in a farmer's dress was walking along a lane some ten miles out of London. There was nobody in sight, neither was there a sound audible save the songs of birds, and these filled the air, for it was a bright, cheerful morning in early summer. Suddenly the farmer's hat appeared to rise gently from his head and vanish.

The good man stopped short in most perfect amazement. He put his hand to his head, and turned and looked in all directions with a scared expression not a little amusing. Then an idea seemed to strike him. He had been walking close by the hedge which on one side separated the lane from a field. He scrambled up the bank and over the hedge. As he did so, away went a whole troop of boys, shouting and laughing uproariously. One of their number held the hat, and after him went the farmer in a style the youngster was evidently not prepared for. The booty was quickly thrown away, but the pursuer was not satisfied. He was bent on capturing the culprit, and after a fine run he brought him into a beautiful corner and fixed him completely.

We hear a great talk sometimes of the loveable qualities of boys; we are told of the boldness and courage of boys; but I never yet knew a boy whose courage, somehow or other, didn't ooze out at his fingers' ends when he found himself fairly in the grasp of an

M

avenging power. A boy, in such evil case, is almost invariably, by turns, a bully and a coward. One minute he implores mercy in the most abject terms, and in the next he hints (if there should be the least chance of the hint availing) at vengeance swift and terrible at the hands of a father or "big brother," or some potent person who may not be expected to be very particular as to on which side the wrong lay. So this bright youth, being now in the ill-used farmer's power, begged forgiveness, and suggested awful retaliation in the same breath.

"Oh, I beg your pardon, I do indeed, I'll tell my father, and, I am very sorry, you'll see what he'll do if you dare touch me."

"For the matter of that, young master, I don't care who interferes. However, I'll let you off this time, though it aint the first, you know; but the next time, why, all I say is—you look sharp;" and with just a gentle shake and a significant look, the farmer scrambled back into the road and resumed his journey.

Now, you would hardly have thought it possible, but that thorough young scoundrel felt himself mightily aggrieved even by this mild admonition. For you see, reader, the boy was the squire's only son; the farmer was one of the squire's tenants; that made all the difference, you know. The boy waited until the farmer had proceeded some yards, and then he picked up a heavy stone, and hurled it at the luckless man with all his force. The stricken man made no effort at pursuit this time. Bleeding from a great gash at the side of the head, he sat down, sick and giddy; while the vile youngster, alarmed at what he had done, and yet without good feeling enough either to render assistance, or even to fetch help, ran home as fast as he could.

The affair caused some noise, but neither punishment ensued to the boy nor compensation to the man; for the squire could not bring his mind to understand that any wrong could be inflicted by his son on a man who was simply a tenant of a small farm; and the man (seeing, perhaps,—who can tell?—a reasonable difficulty in the matter), finding that justice did not respond, called not upon her a second time, and resigned himself to bandages and a low diet.

Years passed, and the wretched specimen of gentle blood was a young man. He had become a terror to his father (he had scarcely another relative), and a terror to the neighbourhood. His extravagancies had seriously crippled the estate; debts and encumbrances were accumulating, creditors were grumbling, friends withdrawing, acquaintances vanishing. Hints went freely round that the squire's day drew to a close, and a great storm would end it. With the farmer, on the other hand, things had prospered. He was almost the only old tenant left; but he remained, in spite of continued exactions and shortcomings on the part of his landlord, and petty affronts from his landlord's son. He loved his little farm which he had held so long, and go he would not, unless they actually turned him out,

And he was turned out at last.   Such utter folly was inexplicable; but notice to quit was served, and the farmer prepared to leave.   In sheer pity, the good man tried to see his landlord and expostulate with him; but while he was yet in the hall of the house the vagabond of a son saw him, and, seizing him by the collar, would have hurled him from the street door, down the stone steps, and perhaps have killed him, had the rake's arm been equal to the lusty farmer's.   But, though it was easy for the farmer to save himself from bodily injury, he was galled by this crowning insult.

"Young man," he said, " I know, as there is a Heaven above us, you will repent this."

"Be off, you old psalm-singer; you canting knave," roared the reprobate; "and be thankful I haven't had the life of you."

"I am thankful, for your sake," was the calm reply; "but mark you, young sir, twice you and I have come together in this way, and twice I've suffered evil at your hands.   If we meet a third time, beware!   So surely as we do, so surely shall I be avenged."

PART II.

A poor man fell near to Bramblestone Workhouse in a fit.   He was taken into the house, and humanely cared for; for the new Poor Law was administered tenderly at Bramblestone.   Next day Mr. Jones, the Relieving Officer, reported the case to the Board.

"He is scarcely sensible yet, poor fellow," said Mr. Jones; "and the doctor doubts his getting over it, for he is quite an elderly man. From his style of dress and general appearance, I should think he was some one who had seen much better days. I have not been able to learn anything from him at present; but his name is doubtless Thomas Eldred, as that is marked on all his linen."

After the Board had broken up, Mr. Zachariah Smith, one of the guardians, came to the Relieving Officer, and said, with some emotion,

" I must see that Thomas Eldred, Mr. Jones. If you are going into the house, perhaps you'll take me to him. I think I know the man."

The official conducted the guardian to the infirmary, and brought him to the bedside of one of the many sufferers the dreary room contained. Mr. Jones did not scan the guardian's countenance as Mr. Smith bent over the lowly couch; but we may, reader; and we may read there mingled emotions of surprise, and deep, deep pity, such as must have had some very unusual source.

" It is as I thought, Mr. Jones," said the guardian, in a low tone. "There can be no objection to my removing this poor fellow to my house?"

The Relieving Officer stared, as well he might. Mr. Zachary Smith was one of the most thriving men in the town. He was an agricultural implement maker; and, having devised some improvements in certain tools, he had prospered considerably. And he deserved all his good fortune, for he was a truly benevolent man, and all the town loved him. But this was certainly a startling fancy,—to move a sick " casual" into his own house.

"It can be done, sir," responded Mr. Jones; "but"—

"There, Mr. Jones, forgive me. All I want to know is, that it is not against rules. For the rest, however odd and inconvenient the proceeding may appear, I am bent upon it. I have known this Thomas Eldred in days gone by. Under my roof, and not under that of a workhouse, shall he now find shelter. I will remove him, please, immediately."

And accordingly the poor sick man was conveyed to Mr. Smith's residence, and there for days life hesitated, so to speak, whether to go or stay. At length consciousness returned. Mr. Smith was sitting not far from the bedside of the sick man, but was partially concealed by a high chair.

The sufferer raised himself, and looked about the room in feeble amazement, as those who have only just returned to the things of the world generally do. He was quite at a loss evidently as to what had come to pass with him (well he might be, indeed), and sunk back, murmuring :—

"I was walking along some road, surely; and now—where can I possibly be? What has happened to me? What friend has brought me here?"

"I am right glad to hear you speak," said Mr. Smith, advancing. "But now lie down again a bit. You are in good quarters and friendly hands."

The sick man gazed earnestly at the benevolent face that met his view, and complied with the injunction; but the next minute he rose again hastily.

"I can't be mistaken. That is Zachariah Smith's face, and that is his voice. I recollect both well. Smith, is it possible that under your roof I have found shelter?"

"I was in hope you would not have known me just now," answered Mr. Smith, cheerfully. "Well, yes, Mr. Eldred, sure enough this is my house, and though I am sorry you should need shelter from any one, yet right pleased am I that you should be here rather than anywhere else."

"Anywhere else!" repeated the sick man, in a tone of despair. "No other place would give me shelter but the grave, Mr. Smith. I'm a beggar, you know, of course—I've not a shilling left—all gone, all gone."

"Bless me!" exclaimed the host, much concerned.

"No. I have not heard tidings of the old place for some time, and though I knew things had not gone well, I was not aware they had gone so ill as that. Of course I was aware—aware of——"

"Reuben's having ruined me and himself—brought shame and disgrace upon us both—and driven me—"

"There, I am wrong in continuing this conversation," interposed Mr. Smith. "You mustn't utter another word. A few days hence we'll talk all this over."

And when the invalid had recovered his strength somewhat, so they did. It was a deplorable story. It was actually the case. Mr. Eldred was utterly destitute. His son had robbed and defrauded him in every possible way; and when his father was penniless, had ventured to cheat other people. This style of acting soon brought things to a crisis. He had to fly the spot, and his poor father, who was rather singularly placed in the non-possession of any relatives, save a few quite remote, and whose friends had of late years completely vanished, quickly followed, reckless whither he went, or what became of him, so ashamed was he and broken-hearted. And now here he was, sheltered beneath the roof of the man whom he, years back, had driven forth from the house and home he had loved so much!

"Stay here awhile," urged the returner of good for evil. "I am a lone man. I have scarcely a relative in the world, and get dull at times. Be in no hurry to go, Mr. Eldred. Your remaining will be quite as much service to me as to yourself."

The time had gone by for pride with poor Mr. Eldred. If he refused the offer, where could he go? He had neither money nor friends. This home abandoned, and there was literally only the Workhouse as a refuge. So the stricken man remained a long, long time—aye, years, reader. And they were about the happiest years his life had known, except, perhaps, a few quite at the out-set. The two men, thus strangely again brought to-gether, grew to regard each other with the warmest feelings. Brotherly love isn't always much worth talk-ing about. The affection which sprung up between Thomas Eldred and Zachariah Smith is worth both talk-ing about and writing about, so constant was it, earnest and sincere.

One evening Zachariah Smith was returning from a long journey. He was passing through "the Valley Field,"—a narrow strip with a high bank on each side, when he came suddenly on a man lolling against a tree, and, as he did so, carefully examining the lock of a pistol. To say the truth, it was not quite a sight which the worthy tradesman cared to see in that place and at that hour. However, he went boldly on, and stared steadily into the man's face. He started back. The man was Reuben Eldred. The recognition was mutual. Eldred first spoke.

"You still alive!" he said fiercely. "You ought to have been under the turf long ago."

"Yes, alive, and willing to aid you, Reuben Eldred, in any way in my power."

"Keep your offers to yourself," was the churlish response. "I'd much rather give you some food I've got here," he said, tapping the pistol significantly, "than take any food from you. Look out for yourself, Master Smith."

"That kind of speech goes for nothing with me," answered Zachariah. "You may shoot me, but you shall first understand I owe you no grudge for the past. I merely wish to lead you to a better future."

"What are you prating about? Hang your impudence! What business have you to talk to me of a better future? How do you know my present is not so delightful, and so beautifully religious, and good, and amiable, you pious Mr. Zachariah Smith, that a better future is not out of the question, eh?"

"I know you've done worse, Reuben Eldred, than even any enemy could have predicted; and I don't gather much ground for believing in any improvement, seeing the occupation in which I have found you."

"Now, to the devil with you, Farmer Smith. It's a nice, pleasant occupation. I like everything that gives me power. Only think now, I've only to put this little machine in that direction, towards your head, an l make a little movement with my finger, and—Oh, pray be off, you old hypocrite, I did wrong to tempt myself with so pleasing a picture as you lying doubled up in the ditch there."

"Shame on you, you miserable reprobate!" replied Zachariah, indignantly. "I will go, indeed, for it's wasting time to implore you to be merciful enough to think of yourself. But one word before you go—Beware! I know of your courses, or, at least, connecting what I know with what I see, I can well divine them. Beware of practising them in Bramblestone. I tell you solemnly, the first lawless deed committed by you here will bring you to the gallows. Think of my words, and may God turn your heart, you wretched man."

Vagabond as he was, Reuben Eldred nevertheless was for a moment staggered with this address, and in that moment Zachariah had passed him, and turning a corner, was out of sight.

In pity, Smith refrained from telling the elder Eldred of the above meeting, and hoped that nothing would bring the son across the father's path. But a meeting was to take place between the two—a final one, and thus it happened :—

Mr. Smith, it has been said, prospered since he came to Bramblestone. He lived in a large, well-furnished house, a little out of the main street. One night, he rose hastily, with the conviction that robbers were in the house. He groped his way to Mr. Eldred's room, and roused him. The two crept to the top of the stairs. There was no doubt about it. Noises below proved the presence of intruders. Neither Mr. Smith nor Mr. Eldred were armed.

"I've a brace of pistols in my room," whispered the farmer. "I'll fetch them." And he went to his bed-room accordingly, leaving his companion on the stair-case. The pistols were not very ready to hand, and a minute or two elapsed before Mr. Smith returned to where he had quitted Mr. Eldred. To his surprise he found the latter had disappeared.

"Never mind," thought Mr. Smith. "Though I've got to fight the battle alone, I'll have a tussle before my chattels shall be made off with," and he cautiously de-scended the stairs.

He listened. The noise was still proceeding. The burglars were evidently bursting locks. The sturdy tradesman grasped his pistols, and felt decidedly blood-thirsty. Still descending, Mr. Smith was not a little surprised to observe the parlour door wide open, and Mr. Eldred standing in the entrance like a statue. Alarmed for his friend—for he foresaw that the robbers, of whom there were four in the room, and who had a lanthorn, might at any moment perceive, and be exceedingly enraged on perceiving how closely they were being watched,— Mr. Smith crept to his companion, and touched his arm anxiously.

Strange! Mr. Eldred moved not in the least.

"For Heaven's sake don't stand there," he whispered; "there are four of them. We must get help."

He had scarcely concluded, when what he feared took place. The robbers saw them. An angry curse issued from the lips of all four simultaneously.

"Blow the old fool's brains out," roared one; and immediately a pistol-shot brought a close to poor Thomas Eldred's long and troubled life. In one point of view it was a merciful shot, friend reader; for what happiness could have remained to that existence when the father had actually discovered among the midnight robbers his lost son, Reuben?

Mr. Smith discharged both of his pistols together, and with effect; for two of the men dropped, while the other two sought escape through the window.

"One of you I'll have," muttered Zachariah, "or you shall kill me before you get away;" and he threw himself violently upon the man who had shot his poor companion.

There was a desperate struggle; but it was shorter than might have been anticipated, for the tradesman, though old, was healthy and strong,—and the robber, though young, was sickly and thin.

"Merciful Heaven!" exclaimed the victor, as the latter's features came into view, "Reuben Eldred!"

"I knew you. I knew you, you scoundrel farmer," yelled the miserable creature. "I—I thought I'd done for you. Surely, I saw you drop. You must be wounded, you know. Eh?—desperately bad. Say you are, you old villain, and I'll go quietly to the lock-up."

"Come here and see who's wounded," was the old man's reply; and he dragged the felon to his victim's side.

"See," said he, putting the lanthorn near; "do you know that face? Look at it well."

"Lord! my father!"

"Yes; your father, Reuben Eldred—his heart broken by you—his life taken by you. Reuben, are you now content? Wretched young man, say 'Lord' again, but this time say it on your knees. Say, 'Good Lord, have mercy on me!' Say it again and again, Reuben Eldred. You have despised every warning, and judgment has fallen upon you. In mercy to yourself, seek God's mercy."

XIV.—MR. JONES IN A LITTLE DIFFICULTY.

BRAMBLESTONE was vexed to hear that Widow Livelight had accepted Mr. Bullwig, the guardian; for Mrs. Livelight was respected, and Mr. Bullwig was not. But then what brought the two together was, that each had what the other wanted. Mrs. Livelight had yet left some tolerable remains of beauty, possessed considerable stores of information, and was a very pleasant and agreeable woman. Mr. Bullwig was a remarkable-looking man,—remarkable through sheer ugliness (ugliness for which one by no means seemed inclined to forgive him, because his unfavourable physiognomy was of a character that augured badly of the inner man), and he was about as cross-grained and ill-tempered a person as ever made good people miserable. But then Mr. Bullwig was rich. He had not long come from Australia, and had brought home a moderate fortune. Mrs. Livelight was fond of money; and when Bullwig made love to her, she never looked at him, but fixed her mental eye upon the figures in his cash-book. So at last she accepted him; and, as I have said, Bramblestone was vexed.

No person in the parish was more annoyed than Mr. Jones, the Relieving Officer. Having long intimately known Mrs. Livelight, he did his best to dissuade her from the union, but to no purpose. The day was fixed for the wedding, and preparations for rejoicing went on actively.

One afternoon, some ten days before the proposed marriage, Mr. Jones was returning, through a country lane, from rather a long round.   A heavy rain coming on unexpectedly is an annoyance to most pedestrians, and a pelting shower caused Mr. Jones to run for shelter to a certain corner of the lane where he knew there was a thick hedge.   At that spot he found, driven there by the same stress, Mrs. Livelight.   The widow plunged at once into the topic which Mr. Jones would have avoided.

"This day fortnight will find me far enough from here, I suppose, Mr. Jones," said Mrs. Livelight, in a melancholy tone, which would have been very appropriate if she had been a worn-out captive in a dungeon acquainting her dear friend with the day of her execution.

"I'm sure I trust it will be a fine day," was Mr. Jones' very prosaic reply.   "It rains fast now."

Of a truth, the Relieving Officer's conversational capacity seemed just then somewhat under a cloud.

"You see, Mr. Jones," remarked the widow, "I am naturally dull at leaving Bramblestone, where I have lived so many years; isn't that what you would expect?"

"Well, perhaps it is, Mrs. Livelight."

"Has the rain so chilled you that you can't speak in a little more cheerful fashion than that?" inquired the widow, in a tone of some annoyance.   "What in the world's the matter, Mr. Jones?"

"Mrs. Livelight," replied the Relieving Officer, with energy, "I knew John Livelight when you and he were married, twenty years ago."   •

"Well, well; bless me! what of that?" asked the widow, not gratified at her advancing years being thus indirectly thrust at her, when she was about being re-married.

"John Livelight wouldn't have liked Brassy Bullwig, Mrs. Livelight. There, now, forgive me; but you know we cannot agree upon this subject; so, is it worth while for us to discuss it?"

"And why should Mr. Bullwig be so-cried down and disliked, and evil spoken of?" petulantly inquired the widow. "You and I have known each other many years, Mr. Jones. Why should you try and make me unhappy?" and Mrs. Livelight began to think herself an ill-used woman, and felt inclined to cry.

"I don't try to make you unhappy, Mrs. Livelight, I wanted to save you from unhappiness when I used all the influence I had with you against this union. But you would follow your own course."

"Well, I can't conceive why you dislike Brassy," exclaimed Mrs. Livelight.

"Dislike him! Why, now, is there a single person in Bramblestone who will say a good word for him?" exclaimed Mr. Jones, with warmth. "Don't the very boys in the street hate him?"

"He might be a handsomer man, I will admit," said the widow, not quite following Mr. Jones's remark.

"Might be handsomer!" exclaimed the indignant Relieving Officer, "why, Mrs. Livelight, that old monkey you've had so .long is a perfect beauty compared with Brassy Bullwig."

"And I suppose you would say he's a little hasty," continued Mrs. Livelight.

"I would say he's a brute, and nothing less."

"Well, well; Brassy, doubtless, has his defects," admitted the widow, who was not desirous of being too strongly reminded of them lest her resolution should break down, "but he has many virtues, many virtues," and Mrs. Livelight sighed tenderly; whether it was because these virtues, though visible to her, were not visible to the rest of the world, or because they were matters of faith rather than of sight, this narrative cannot record.

"But the rain is nearly over, and——"

"Perhaps Mrs. Livelight would like to take my arm," said Mr. Brassy Bullwig, making his appearance round the corner of the hedge.

The widow screamed, and the Relieving Officer was taken aback. The concentrated malignity manifested in the countenance of the respected Bullwig satisfied Mr. Jones that the whole of the foregoing conversation had been overheard by the person to whom, beyond all others in the world, it would be distasteful. And all doubt on the point was soon removed.

"So, so, Mr. Relieving Officer," cried Brassy; "yes, yes! ah, ah! so, so! ah, well! of course."

N

Now this was not particularly intelligible.   The fact
was, Mr. Bullwig was at the moment rather incon
veniently laden with a downright furious, blood-thirsty
desire to slaughter Mr. Jones on the spot.   He could
with difficulty subdue himself sufficiently to enable him
just to give the luckless official a notion of the vengeance
which would quickly overtake him.   When he did
manage, however, to get speech to flow, he burst forth
with vigour.

"Yes Mr. Relieving Officer perhaps you're right
So there's not a single person in Bramblestone who will
say a good word for me the very boys in the street hate
me I'm a brute and nothing less and you think I'm going
to put up with this you're much mistaken you insulting
scoundrel my name's not Brassy Bullwig if I don't
make you smart you good-for-nothing—Mrs. Livelight
allow me."

Thus singularly running his express train filled with
abuse of Mr. Jones straight into his request to the widow
to let him hold her umbrella, the infuriated Guardian
hurried off, leaving the Poor-Law official, notwithstanding his natural hardihood, rather in consternation at the
mishap which had occurred.

Mr. Jones returned to the Union office.

"That woman Small has been here," said Mr. Flack,
the Assistant Relieving Officer, "and taken her three
and sixpence and two loaves, and when she'd got them,
the hussey, she declared she'd go and buy a bottle of gin
and drink it under Mr. Bullwig's windows."

"Bless my soul!" exclaimed Mr. Jones, "what an omission of mine. Mr. Bullwig this morning countermanded the order to give Small that relief. Didn't I tell you, Mr. Flack? Botheration! I ought to have done so."

When a man tries to throw some blame off his own shoulders by asking you whether it should not be transferred to yours, he hardly expects an answer, and, if you be wise, you will not give him one. Mr. Flack was silent; Mr. Jones mused.

"This is unfortunate," he muttered; "I'll go and tell the whole story to the Chairman." So to his staunch friend, Mr. Eardley, he went. The Chairman was rather sorry for the affair, "but," he remarked, "we have nothing to do, Mr. Jones, as a Board of Guardians, with the first grievance, let Mr. Bullwig say what he may. For the second you must get a scolding, you know—there's no relieving you of that; however, I daresay it won't kill you."

The day of the weekly board meeting was two days afterwards. The Board assembled, all but Mr. Bullwig. It was evident that some communication had passed from that gentleman to several of the Guardians, for there was a whispering, accompanied by ominous looks at the Relieving Officer, which could not be unobserved. Business commenced, and some interesting cases were investigated. One man was had in who had supported six human beings on a shilling a day for some weeks past. The curiosity of the Guardians was excited, and they thought they would like to see these human beings. Well, there was no difficulty; they were only outside in the passage, and were speedily introduced. Strange to say, they were all very clean; there was nothing in the least degree repulsive about them; but they had to be handled very tenderly lest they should be pulled to pieces; and fortunately there was not a strong draught in the room, or they might have floated about the heads of the Guardians, and that, too, without there being anything mysterious in the performance, or furnishing food for scientific inquiry.

Then there was quite a different case. The entry of two applicants, a man and his wife, caused the immediate departure of the like number of Guardians to the inn hard by, to beg a small glass of the best brandy as quickly as it could be procured. Strange to say, that which contact with these unfortunates had forced these Guardians to seek, was the cause to which the ill-starred creatures owed their appearance there. Mr. Jones soon told their story—"They were always drinking and always starving." They didn't deny it. It was all down-hill with them, and would never be up-hill again in this world.

The Board had just consigned the man to the stone-yard and the woman to the wash-tub, when an alarming sound was heard. It seemed, literally, as though every pane of glass in the office window had been smashed with one blow. The Guardians rose in consternation. The bell was rung and Mr. Flack summoned. That

diminutive gentleman appeared, looking very hot and
excited. He burst out at once—

"What to make of her I'm sure I can't tell, gentlemen. It is the most remarkable story *ever* I heard—I
say it is the most remarkable, the most——"

"Mercy on us, Mr. Flack!" interposed the Chairman.
"Take it coolly, man—what's it all about? Is somebody
going to pull the place down about our ears?"

"Ah, but you can't imagine, Mr. Eardley——"

"My good man, I don't want to imagine, I want to
learn——"

"The most remarkable thing—the most remarkable,
I say—the most——"

"He's certainly gone crazy," observed the Chairman,
in a half-pitying tone. "Here, Mr. Jones, will you
just step out and quickly gather, if you can, what has
happened; and let the doctor see Mr. Flack at once, or
he'll have brain fever. It is the most remarka——
pshaw! I'm talking the same nonsense myself."

Out went the Relieving Officer, and was absent fully
five minutes. Then he returned, almost as flushed as
Mr. Flack had been.

"Well," he said, "if it's true, it certainly is the
most remarkable—"

But here a general outcry stopped him, and he gave
an explanation to the Board which created considerable
surprise.

"Better have the woman in, I think," said the Chairman, looking round.

No one dissenting, a tall, ferocious person was ushered in. She was beyond middle age, very meanly dressed, and seemed in a most desperate mind.

"You may do what you like with me—I don't care," she cried, directly she entered the room.

"Answer quietly my questions, and I think you will receive some benefit," said Mr. Eardley. "You say your name is——"

"How many more times am I to be teased about my name! Bridget Bullwig is my name, once more and for the last time."

"Very well; you shan't be asked again. And where is it you've just come from?"

"Bother. What! All this over again, too. Australia."

"Yes; well, and you're married?"

"Would you like to dispute it, you or any of you?"

"Most certainly not."

"Of course, I'm married. Mr. Brassy Bullwig's my husband. Oh, but he's a cruel man. I was laid up with the fever over there, and he left me—left me without a farthing. He thought I should die, no doubt; but I didn't. I recovered; and, when I found out he'd come to England, said I, 'I'll follow him. I'll be down upon him.' Because, you see, he married me when he was well nigh starving, and I was the better off of the two; for I was servant in a good place. When he found gold and made money I wasn't fit for him, and he wanted to get rid of me. O, the villain! I'll find him yet. I should know him among ten thousand, and he shall see; he *shall* see——''

" Well, now, my good woman, wait a minute. You go quietly with this gentleman, and it's possible that in a few minutes I will be able to tell you something about your lost husband."

The " good woman" uttered a cry of delight, and submitted immediately to Mr. Jones, who placed her, under guardianship, in a room close at hand. He had scarcely returned when Mr. Brassy Bullwig arrived.

Mr. Bullwig glowed with self-importance as usual, but seemed in a tolerably good humour. He nodded and smiled around, and took his seat. Then he rose, and proceeded with his lighter indictment against Mr. Jones, that referring to neglect of orders. Mr. Jones admitted his fault, and was duly admonished.

"Well, now, gentlemen," said Mr. Bullwig, with something of the air of a prizefighter who has been defied by a butcher's boy, and is about to inflict vengeance, " that which I am about to mention will, through the awful depravity, the appalling baseness, the inconceivable blackness of coal—I should say soul—which it will show—I should say exhibit—carry conviction to your most internal sensations."

Mr. Bullwig, wishing to create a most unusual effect, had with much care prepared this powerful exordium, and now delivered it with terrible impressiveness. The orator then proceeded to detail the circumstances of his second indictment, with which the reader is acquainted.

"Gentlemen," he said, in conclusion, "what might have been the awful consequences of this man's baseness! He might have turned from me a love without which I could not live. He might have deprived me of a tender, affectionate wife, who, within a few days from this time, will bring me all the comfort and happiness which her many virtues are capable of bestowing—who——"

"Upon my word—forgive me for interrupting," interposed Mr. Eardley—"I don't see how exactly Mr. Jones could have done all this, had he been the greatest scoundrel in existence. The fact is, we've had Mrs. Bullwig here this morning."

"Mrs. Bullwig, Mr. Eardley! Eh, sir! What do you mean, sir? Why, the wedding isn't till Thursday. What is—eh! what do you all mean?" cried the alarmed Brassy, not liking the looks of those around him.

"Here comes the lady," said the Chairman; and Mrs. Bullwig, escorted by Mr. Jones, entered the room.

A moment, and all doubt of the truth of her story had vanished. It was difficult to say which was loudest,— the lady's cry of exultation, or the gentleman's yell of despair. That very unpleasant thing, "a scene," ensued; but ultimately the parties were induced to withdraw, and order was restored. Mr. Bullwig speedily departed from Bramblestone with his dear wife, and Mrs. Livelight obtained some of his property notwithstanding, for a commiserating jury applied a verdict of £1000 as a solace to her woes.

XV.—THE.BEDRIDDEN PAUPER.

"So, our neighbour, Mr. Weldon, is leaving us," I said to Mr. Jones.

"Yes, and joy go with him," was the short reply.

"That seems to imply you are not over-anxious for his remaining," I observed. "Why, he's one of your guardians, is he not?"

"There's nothing particularly bad about the man," said the Relieving Officer, in a tone by no means complimentary; "but Weldon has never been the same man since his disappointment that he was before. That soured him for life."

"What was it? It must have been something before my time."

"Haven't you heard that story, sir? There was an immense deal of talk about it years ago."

"No; I'm quite ignorant. Tell me all about it."

"Some years back, sir, there lived, at the large red house which stands at the entrance of the town, an odd old gentleman, named Tasker. He was a bachelor, seventy years of age, and to all appearance had not a relative living. He was very rich; but his expenditure must have been quite trifling, for he kept no company, and though now and then he was seized with a liberal fit (and when the fit was on him gifts flowed from him freely enough, it must be owned), as a rule he was very

parsimonious.   Amongst his few intimate acquaintances
was Mr. Weldon.   For Mr. Weldon the old gentleman
manifested as much regard as his nature was capable of,
and I need scarcely say that, under the circumstances,
our neighbour was not slow to strengthen and confirm
the partiality.   The pair were constantly together, Mr.
Tasker, however, being at Mr. Weldon's house ten times
for once that Mr. Weldon was at Mr. Tasker's ; and the
Bramblestonians looked and laughed, and, to say the
truth, hated Weldon most cordially for the advantages
which seemed likely to accrue to him in respect of this
singular friendship.   It was openly asserted that Tasker's
property brought him a clear two thousand a-year, and
it was as openly predicted that every farthing would
become Weldon's at the old gentleman's death.

Of this latter event looming in the distance the old
gentleman himself seemed to think very little.   I confess
I used to fancy when Weldon was asked after his friend
Mr. Tasker's health, that it was only with half-concealed
chagrin he used to reply, "Wonderful, sir, wonderful ;
the worthy man will fight the common enemy for years
yet."   I thought to myself, "It's lucky for the old gentleman that 'the common enemy' cannot make a friend
of you as against his prey in this case, Mr. Weldon ;
the battle would soon be over, if he could, and the victim
be secured in no time."

There was one point, however, and a very important
one, which continually weighed upon the minds of the
Weldon family, and it was this.   Although with them

Mr. Tasker grew more and more friendly daily, while from other society he proportionately withdrew himself, still he never hinted in the least as to his having made a will. As young Weldon and the two Miss Weldons once said, somewhat indiscreetly, in my hearing, "This was very vexing, for really they hardly knew they had father or mother; they hardly knew they had a home; they hardly knew, even, they had tastes, thoughts, dispositions, which they could call their own, so completely did the Tasker spirit override everybody and everything in the Weldon house, and so abjectly did all wills and ways in that house fall prostrate before the one disagreeable but much respected influence. And, after all, it was but speculation. Pa might be wrong; the old gentleman might mean nothing," and so forth.

But my impression, sir, is, that at that time "Pa" was not wrong, and that whether Mr. Tasker had or had not made a will, he certainly intended to leave every sixpence of his property to the Weldons. They had him completely to themselves, they courted and humoured him, they made themselves slaves to him, as I have said, and in common gratitude I do believe the old gentleman would have largely enriched them, if not in his lifetime, at all events at his death, but for— Sophy Simpkins.

One day Mr. Weldon and Mr. Tasker came to the Workhouse.

"Have a walk round the wards with me," said the

Guardian to his companion, "you'll be interested for the few minutes it will occupy you."

Mr. Tasker rather drew back. His customary parsimony clung closely to him at that moment.

"No, never mind, I'll wait for you," he replied; "I—I'd rather not be asked for money. These—these paupers always want money; very odd, and very disagreeable."

Even the surly Weldon smiled contemptuously at this exhibition of liberality.

"Bless you, no, sir, they would no more dare ask you for anything than they would throw themselves out of window. The idea of a pauper asking for anything indeed. We have stone-yards, wash-tubs, and oakum-rooms, strong-rooms and refractory-wards, my dear sir, all perfect. It's quite a treat to see them."

"Daresay—no doubt," was the half-pettish reply, "but I'd rather not; you go, I'll wait."

So as it was his duty that day to inspect the house, Mr. Weldon went with me, and Mr. Tasker was left in the ante-room.

My companion was not a favourite with the paupers. Rough speech and rough usage they invariably met with at his hands.

"So you're still idling away the time here, Wilkins," was his greeting to the very first pauper who met his eye.

Now, the man was breaking stones with an energy which caused the perspiration to ooze from him at every pore. I believe he had been required to break so much stone previous to his dinner, and although the dinner would that day be only soup and bread, yet to a strong fellow of six-and-twenty, the attraction of any food, after a long fast, had imparted a vigour almost preternatural.

"Idling, do ye call it?" exclaimed the ill-starred Wilkins, displaying a face purple with his excessive exertion, and damp as though it had been dipped in a pail of water and imperfectly dried with a mop. "Idling, d'ye call it?—then there now (throwing down his hammer), blow'd if I'll do any more."

"Please yourself, by all means," coolly observed Mr. Weldon.

"I'll starve," roared the unfortunate.

"Do your work, sir, and hold your tongue."

"I'm a good mind to lay down on them stones and die." (A slight movement towards the hammer.)

"Again I say, please yourself by all means."

"Bless'd if this isn't hawful," groaned poor Wilkins, resuming the hammer. "Talk of niggers, why a West Ingee nigger in his plantin is a prince to this ere English free-born pauper a stone-breakin—blow'd!" And with this bitter, though not very clearly defined reflection, the strong arms went up again, again the heap of stones was stricken, and again the begrimed face grew purple, and the perspiration oozed out. "Ah, sir, hunger's a wonderfully thick whip."

Plenty of other paupers were rated. One would have

thought (hearing Mr. Weldon's addresses to them) that Bramblestone Workhouse was a palace, and that through sheer love of ease and good living a lot of idlers and pleasure-seekers had taken up their abode there, to their shame and disgrace. I am glad to say, sir, I have known few Guardians like Mr. Weldon. They do a world of mischief. Bad enough it is for an honest but unfortunate man to have to come into the House, but so long as heart and hope remain, no great harm is done. It is when you have driven his self-respect from him by coarse reproaches, which he knows to be unjust but cannot resent, that you run the risk of ruining the man for life. The wretched comfort of intoxication is never more fascinating than when it beckons to a poor brow-beaten spirit. The paupers in the parish of which Weldon was Guardian were the most incorrigible in the Union. He made them so—I say he made them so—that harsh, tyrannising, unchristian man.

But I beg your pardon. Now to my story. Well, we had gone through the wards, and I had opened the door of the infirmary, which was always inspected last, when Mr. Weldon started, and exclaimed—

"Mercy on me, why there's Tasker!"

And so there was. The old gentleman stood at about the middle of the room, both his hands on his forehead and his face ashy pale.

Mr. Weldon ran up to him.

"What, Tasker?" he cried, "what is it, what is wrong? you here, why, eh!"

"Yes, yes, quite right," replied his friend, turning aside hurriedly; "a little faint, quite right now. There, let me be," he added, half petulantly; and he tottered out of the room.

The Guardian and I stood in mute surprise. Then we each cast a searching glance round the room. Mr. Weldon's eye dropped. He saw nothing. My more practised eye detected a clue to the mystery.

The Guardian was not a good tactician. He could be roughly agreeable, but of delicate kindness he had no more than a hyena. When we had rejoined Mr. Tasker, Mr. Weldon pressed and worried him about his illness till the old gentleman nearly quarrelled with him. He had become tired of waiting, he insisted, and had strolled after us, and had wandered into the infirmary. There the air of the place and the sights around had sickened him. Surely we might understand that.

Satisfactory or not, nothing more could be elicited, so the friends departed, neither in the best of tempers.

What had been unusual in the Infirmary? I had seen a face usually pale as the face of the dead, flushed and crimsoned as with strong wine. In the Infirmary lay a poor woman who had been there for years. She was hopelessly paralyzed. She had no friends or relatives that could be found, and in this sad room, lodged and fed by unwilling charity, and tended by hardened hirelings, she seemed destined to lie waiting for many years yet the summons to arise and go hence. Yet it was the face of Sophy Simpkins, thus strangely changed,

that my eye had remarked, when I sought an explanation, which I felt sure was somewhere about, by Mr.
Tasker's emotion.

My impression was confirmed.   In the afternoon of
that day Mr. Tasker came to me.   His trembling hand
was upon my shoulder, as he said in a husky, quivering
voice—

" Mr. Jones, you must do something for me—secretly, mind, secretly—and God will bless you."

" It has reference to Sophy Simpkins," I said quietly.

" Mercy!   What do you know? How do you guess ?"
he inquired in alarm.   " Has she——"

" Be quite at ease, Mr. Tasker. I only surmise. Now
what can I do ?"

" Simply take this money " (and he put a heavy purse
into my hand) " and remove Sophy Simpkins to a quiet,
but comfortable lodging in the neighbourhood."

" I must get the Board's permission," I answered.
" Am I to mention your request ?"

" Dear,—dear no," he answered.   " Say—say—a
friend, yes, a friend, who has bound you to secresy, has
asked you to undertake this.   You shall come into no
trouble, you shall not, indeed, Mr. Jones.   You shall be
well recompensed.   Say you will do it—but speedily,
and, above all, mind—secretly, secretly."

I scarcely wished to be mixed up with any mysterious proceeding, but in helping to relieve the Union of a
bedridden pauper there could be no possible harm, and
moved by the old man's earnestness, I consented.   The

next Board day I intimated that some friend of Sophy Simpkins, who desired to remain unknown, requested leave to remove her to a lodging in the neighbourhood, and had furnished me with the means of carrying out their wish. Some curiosity was manifested by the Guardians, (Mr. Weldon was not present), but I said frankly I could not gratify it, and permission was given.

Sophy was conveyed forthwith to a humble but pleasant apartment just out of the town, and a nurse was hired to be with her. She manifested no surprise, though some satisfaction, when I informed her of her intended removal, and I carefully abstained from showing the least curiosity as to the causes which had led to Mr. Tasker's interference in her favour.

Although Mr. Weldon heard of Sophy Simpkins's removal under these peculiar circumstances, he, rather strangely, never made any remark to me on the subject, and I think any connection between Mr. Tasker's illness and the bettered condition of the poor bedridden woman never suggested itself to his mind. I believe her benefactor scarcely ever visited Sophy. It was always dark when he called on her (once in four months or thereabouts), and occasionally I understood from the nurse (a discreet, silent woman), he required to be left alone in the cottage, with Sophy. No wonderment, no joke or little tattle went forth in the town. So well was the secret preserved, that I question whether it ever passed beyond the four persons immediately concerned in it.

Mr. Weldon and Mr. Tasker soon grew friendly again.

o

The Weldon family even increased their painful efforts
.to secure the exclusive regard of the old gentleman, and,
to all appearance, they succeeded.

So about two years went over. Sophy Simpkins still
lived, and Mr. Tasker's secret was still preserved. Then
the invalid became much worse, and freedom from that
long, long bondage was near at hand.

I could see, by Mr. Tasker's anxious and concerned
looks, that this circumstance was weighing upon and
distressing him. Quite an old man now, he was incapable of bearing long any trouble, particularly any concealed trouble, and the Weldon family began to shake
their heads, and think of a suitable inscription for their
old friend's tombstone.

One night late I went to the cottage where Sophy
Simpkins lay. It was, as I have said, a little out of
Bramblestone, away from other houses. I tried the
door, which, like the doors of all country cottages, was
usually only on the latch, and found it fastened. I
knew by this that Mr. Tasker was alone with Sophy,
so I let the latch fall gently, and withdrew.

I had scarcely turned aside when I saw the nurse knock
at the door of the cottage. She was admitted, and Mr.
Tasker came out. He passed me without seeing me,
apparently, and I preferred not to stop him. I entered
the cottage, and spoke to the nurse.

She put her finger to her lips. "Very bad," she
whispered; "she frightens me." And the woman
looked pale and scared.

"Just left," I whispered in response, alluding to Mr. Tasker.

The nurse nodded, and muttered, "As bad as she is—both, before long," and she pointed to the ground. "Do you mind taking charge of her for a few minutes while I go into the town?" she asked.

This was a little service I often rendered, so I made no objection now, and simply desiring her not to be longer than she could help, I took my seat and the nurse departed.

She had been gone about five minutes. I was impatient for her return, and moving restlessly I overturned the candlestick, and the light was extinguished. It was late in autumn, but the weather being very warm there was no fire in the cottage, so that I now sat in nearly total darkness. I did not move, for I knew not where to find the means of relighting the candle, and so I simply, with increased impatience, waited the nurse's return.

So long as I live, sir, I shall never forget the start I gave on feeling suddenly, as I thus sat, a hand cold as the hand of a corpse placed upon my forehead. I had heard not a sound previously. The bedridden and dying woman in the next room I believed to be utterly incapable for years of standing erect even for a moment. In the name of everything wonderful, whose hand was upon me?

"Sit still," said a low voice.

"Mercy on me!" I cried. "Is that you, Sophy?

How have you left your bed?" and I rose and grasped the form before me.

I scarcely expect you'll believe me, sir, but it certainly seeemed to me, that, with a strength beyond my own, I was pressed down again in my chair. I remember vividly, even now, my heart beating as though it would burst from me, and the cold perspiration oozing from my forehead. I strained my eyes, but there was not a glimmer of light, and I could not see a single thing.

"The time has come," said Sophy's voice. "I told him it was not far off, and he laughed at me."

"What in the world are you talking about, Sophy?" I inquired, striving to speak in a bold tone, but failing miserably, I know well.

"There he is, I say, there he is," she almost shrieked.

"Where, where?" I cried aghast, peering through the darkness.

"Where? Why, *here*. I hold him! I hold him!" and she clutched me fiercely with both hands.

"Henry," said the poor creature, who thus, in her dying hour, must have for a few minutes wonderfully recovered her bodily at the cost of losing her mental faculties—"Henry, let it come now. I'll ward it off no longer. Here—now—be with me. You shall not go—I say you shall not go."

She clutched me round the neck convulsively. Scared, I confess, and alarmed, I tried to release myself, telling her who I was, and begging her to find her way back to her bedroom, while I sought means of relighting the candle. But her only reply was the grasping me more tightly, so that I was almost suffocated.

A bright light shone in the room. Aghast, I struggled to my feet. A broad sheet of flame, blinding and scorching, and a shriek of pain and consternation bewildering me, I fell back stupefied. The room was on fire. In an instant we were quite enveloped in flame. Whether the candle had fallen on some easy ignitable substance, and the fire, after smouldering for a minute or so, had burst widlly forth, I cannot tell. That is the only conjecture I can offer. But there was the fierce flame rapidly extending to everything around us, and the thin dress of the poor creature before me was even now on fire.

I recollect, sir, with a feeling of positive awe, suddenly beholding at this terrible moment the face of Mr. Tasker. Yes, there it was, at the door, not bearing an expression, as I have often thought since, of surprise and alarm, but simply ashy pale, as I had seen it in the Infirmary on the well-remembered day. I shouted aloud. I seized my unfortunate companion, and sprung forward to escape through the door. And now comes a mystery. I felt my burden torn from my arms by a violent wrench which nearly threw me back again into the flames. I recovered myself, and dashed into the air. The very next moment the whole cottage succumbed to the flame— the roof fell, and the ruin was complete.

Soon a great crowd gathered. They tossed right and

left the burning beams.   They asked no questions of me, and I was so sick and faint I could scarcely have answered them if they had.   Presently they gave a great shout.

"They have found the bodies," I said eagerly.

"Poor Sophy Simpkins!" was murmured through the crowd.   And I saw them drag *something* through the crowd, and gather round it.   Then I fainted, and was carried into a house in the town.

I soon recovered.   A Relieving Officer, sir, is not much given to fainting.   The people of the house were talking around me in an under-tone.

"It must have been almost at the minute the fire broke out," said one, whose voice revealed her as the housemaid at Mr. Weldon's.   "He dropped like a stone, and all he said was, 'Sophy, where are you?   I want Sophy Simpkins!' and he was quite gone.   They were carrying him upstairs when we heard the alarm of fire."

"Why, who are you talking about?" I inquired.

"Ah! you don't know, Mr. Jones.   Why, of poor Mr. Tasker.   He died suddenly, an hour ago, in a fit."

"Mr. Tasker!   Where?"

"He had just come in to tea with master.   They had talked a little bit, and were sitting quite comfortable, when the old gentleman, all of a sudden, springs from his chair, calls for Sophy Simpkins, and then tumbles on the floor stone dead."

What was this they were telling me.   Had the old man, then, not come to the cottage?   Had I only fancied I saw him? And who had forced Sophy Simpkins from my arms? I know, sir, you will think I must have parted with my senses for awhile on this occasion. But Mr. Tasker I *saw*, and Mr. Tasker I fully believe took Sophy Simpkins from me, and fell with her into the fire. Others, about that same moment, saw him fall and die a quarter of a mile off, calling, however, with his dying breath for the creature who was then gasping in the flames. I cannot explain it, sir. There are the simple facts, and even yet I can scarce think of them without a shudder.

"And about the Weldons, Mr. Jones?"

"There was no will, sir—and the whole family openly gnashed their teeth, and reviled the poor dead, for twelvemonths afterwards. The property went to the crown."

"And was there never any explanation, Mr. Jones, of the strange connection between Mr. Tasker and Sophy Simpkins?"

"Never, sir. It was known that Sophy, in younger life, had been much away from home, and had not been a very discreet damsel. That is all I can say. Poor Sophy—poor Mr. Tasker—they make part of the great company in yonder old churchyard. And their secret is buried with them."

XVI.—THE INFIRMARY VISITOR.

THERE was a short simple story connected with Bramblestone which Mr. Jones, albeit a Relieving Officer, used to relate with much pathos. In Bramblestone churchyard was a tombstone, bearing the inscription of Clara Leslie, died 18th January, 18—, aged 19 years. The story had relation to the young girl who lay there. I will give it as the Relieving Officer told it to me.

Mr. Leslie, sir, was one of the best guardians who ever sat at the Board. Clear-headed and kind-hearted, and with plenty of means, it was a happy thing for the paupers when he agreed to serve an office the very reverse of pleasant. Mrs. Leslie was just like her husband, and was as much beloved. And then there was their daughter Clara—the poor people idolised her, and no wonder.

They were a happy family truly; and I suppose that for years there was not another family in the town so free from sources of discomfort or anxiety as the Leslies. But, of course, this state of things did not last. Troubles must come, sir, to all, and a cloud came over the Leslies.

That dreary room, the Workhouse Infirmary, which has figured more than once in the "Recollections" that have amused you occasionally, will take a prominent

place in my story about Miss Clara Leslie. I call it a
dreary room. It was not so in itself: it was large, well-
lighted, well-arranged, and well-ventilated. But then
sickness and pain always dwelt there, and death was a
constant visitor, so it could not be otherwise than gloomy.

Just the place, sir, and yet not the place, for Miss Clara
Leslie. Just the place, because here was a field for her
kindest, most self-denying labour; not the place—in fact,
the worst place for her, for a peculiar reason. Like so
many of the amiable and good, Miss Leslie was weak
and delicate. At the time of which I am speaking she
was about sixteen years old. She had been nurtured
with great care, and there were as yet no marked signs
in her of the disease which subsequently destroyed her.
Still, the Infirmary was not a place which so tender a
plant could visit, even for a few hours a week, without
injury; and, to say the truth, much as I esteemed the
dear young lady, I was always sorry when I met her in
my journeys round the wards.

But there was another reason, and, perhaps, yet more
important. Like most young persons of delicate consti-
tution, Clara Leslie was very susceptible of strong im-
pressions. The dark scenes she sometimes witnessed,
the sad words uttered in her hearing, did not pass away
from her mind. They remained there as so many sub-
jects of painful thought; and I could see, with singular
distinctness, how completely she was gliding under the
influence of a shadow, which, deepening by degrees,
might ultimately remove her from our sight.

There was one old woman upon whom Miss Clara was a constant attendant, and towards whom, I must confess, I felt no small aversion. Sarah Milton, aged seventy, belonging to one of the outlying parishes, was a life-long invalid, and as such had my sincere pity. But then she was of such a morose, puritanical turn that it was, indeed, up-hill, cheerless work to endeavour to soothe and comfort her by any of that light, hopeful chit-chat generally so useful in cases where weakness is almost the only ailment. Even the chaplain, persevering and con-scientious as he was, held very short communion with Sarah Milton, and passed on to patients more troubled in body, mayhap, but less in mind than this unfortunate but very disagreeable old lady.

Now, what could cause Miss Clara to take a vast fancy to so unpromising a subject is, indeed, a mystery, but at Sarah Milton's bedside oftener than at the bedside of any other patient, certainly, was the kind young lady seen. Perhaps she thought it her duty to pay more attention where it met with least reward. For much the same sort of recognition of goodness was bestowed by Sarah upon her youthful visitor as upon those who, confessedly, would scarcely have gone near her had they not been paid for the duty. I could hear, unceasingly, when the tender-hearted girl was bending over her, trying by every kind expression to animate and encou-rage her, the same miserable whine:

"Thank you, Miss; but please don't talk to me of the wicked world. There are none but sinners, Miss Leslie, and they will all be put into the oven."

Then, perhaps, Miss Clara would reply.:

"Not all, I hope; not one, I would pray."

Upon which the cheerful old lady would groan and shake her head dolefully, and would presently burst out afresh with her conviction touching the oven and its contents.

One day I overheard the following:

"Better to-day, Mrs. Milton, I hope?"

"Shall never be better in this world, Miss Leslie."

"Don't lose heart."

"Miss Leslie, what hope have you?"

"O, I'm young and strong, you know; so I naturally am buoyant."

The old lady laughed scornfully.

"Full of hope," she groaned. "Yes, of course. Why, I see you in your grave, Miss Leslie."

"Eh!" exclaimed her visitor, rather startled.

"I've seen you in your coffin, and looked at you in your grave many a time," continued the invalid.

Miss Leslie was concerned. She thought the old lady must be wandering.

"My poor child!" moaned the afflicted lady, gazing upwards at the beautiful young face with an expression of the deepest woe.

"Why, what is the matter? what has happened?" was the natural inquiry.

"Sin is the matter, and sin has happened," was the rather indefinite reply; "and the oven is heated till it is red hot. Miss Clara Leslie, I'll tell you a dream I've had about you. I saw you lying quietly in your bed—dreaming, no doubt, of the vanities of which youth never have enough. All was still and peaceful. But suddenly I saw something in the room gather and thicken until it became a shape, a dreadful shape. And it bent over you. And I saw your face, which before looked so happy, grow dark and troubled, your arms were thrown wildly out, and your teeth gnashed, and you screamed loudly. Still you did not awake. Then that fearful thing which hovered over you seemed completely to cover as though it would suffocate you. And I came to understand what it was. Miss Clara, it was sin. Sin was thus enveloping you, and grasping you as its prey. But it was foiled. Oh! it was foiled, and my heart leaped for joy. For a light shone in the room; and I saw one like an angel standing by your bed. There was sweet pity on that face, and love. But it was so pale; and as the calm, clear eyes turned towards and rested upon you, I knew the face well; it was a face I have looked for and prayed to see through many a long year—the face of the Angel of Death."

Although I stood at a little distance, listening to all this with some regret, for a special reason, yet I could not help being struck with the accuracy and force of expression to which the suffering woman seemed for the occasion to have attained.

"And Miss Clara, now listen," she resumed, with continued earnestness. "I saw you smile, and you awoke. And your eyes met first that evil thing which still hung near you. Oh! with what horror did I per-

cieve that it created in you no loathing—no anguish.
You rather seemed to invite its companionship. I
thought you would hold out your arms to it. My blood
ran cold. The accursed thing expanded. Another victim—another victim—and one so young and beautiful,
and good and kind! I prayed, Miss Clara, I prayed for
you, and there drew near to you the messenger who had
come to preserve you evermore from harm. Then your
eyes turned to that serene face, and as they did so a
light I cannot describe shone in the room and round
about you, and you seemed to fall asleep a second time.
And the angel's arms were round you, and I knew that
evil and your spirit could never meet again."

"I don't like her talking to Miss Leslie in that
strain," I thought. "The young lady is not well, I am
sure, and if this well-told, but mischievous piece of
imagination fixes itself in her mind, it may do her
much harm." So I interfered.

"Why—what is all this?" I said briskly. "You
had the nightmare, Mrs. Milton, you know. There
was nothing wonderful about it. We mustn't startle
Miss Leslie with accounts of dismal dreams."

I cannot describe the look of ineffable contempt which
was the good lady's only reply to this speech. But
Miss Clara said—

"Yet it was very remarkable, Mr. Jones, was it not?
Ah, the Angel of Death!" she sighed. "The pale face
and pitying eyes——"

"Oh, my dear young lady," I interrupted, "that's

very pretty poetry, but we mustn't indulge much in poetry in a world where there's plenty of work to do. Did I not hear Mr. Leslie was about to give a ball ?"

At this query, the invalid gave a groan which implied her conviction that I had now fairly thrown off the mask, and openly sold myself to the Evil One, and even the young lady put on such a demure look that I did not repeat the question. I was in hope that the latter would have left the Infirmary, but she remained some time longer in conversation with the sick woman, and I was obliged to quit them.

Ah, sir, I have said that, for a special reason, I disliked this kind of conversation being held with Miss Clara. I had long had my misgivings about her health, although none, apparently, had been excited in her parents. In six months from that time she was in her grave.

It was very soon after the foregoing conversation in the Infirmary that Bramblestone rejoiced to hear Miss Leslie was about to be married. She had been engaged for a year or two, and Mr. Leslie thought the wedding might now take place. Mr. John Cartlake, the junior partner in the country bank, was the fortunate man : and he semed every way worthy. He was well-connected, rich, and handsome ; he was good-tempered and pleasant-mannered. It was only at the last moment, when the day had actually been fixed, and the dresses and breakfast had been ordered, it transpired Mr. John Cartlake was something else—he was a great rogue.

He had long defrauded his firm, and he decamped with a large sum of money.

And when I heard this, and contemplated the effect it would produce on Miss Clara, I called to mind old Sarah Milton's dream, and I too had a vision of the Angel of Death.

It was realised. "Miss Clara was ill."—"Miss Clara was, of course, much distressed."—"Miss Clara was ordered change of air."—"Miss Clara seemed to pine sorely." Then the family left Bramblestone for a couple of months. "Miss Clara was dying. They were coming back. She wished to die in the old house."

You see, sir, I have no startling incidents in this story of mine. It is the old, old tale of the young and beautiful, and the disease which seems especially to mark them out and cling to them, and bring them early to their better home. The Leslies returned, and I saw Miss Clara again. She had sent for me; she wanted to ask me about Sarah Milton. Should I tell her? Sarah Milton lay in the churchyard, where the body which contained the young, bright spirit itself lay, a week or two on. The circumstances immediately connected with her death were singular.

One beautiful summer evening I was passing through the churchyard when I heard the organ. I had a friend with me, and remarking to him that our organ was a very fine one, and that the organist appeared to be playing, as was his custom sometimes, for his own gratification, I proposed our entering to listen. We did so.

There was no one in the church, and we took our seats quietly.

It was, indeed, a noble old instrument, and was admirably played. "Glory to God in the highest, peace on earth, and good will towards men." A flood of sound filled every nook and crevice of the venerable building. A feeling of religious enthusiasm took possession of our souls, and raised them to the contemplation of pure and lofty things in Heaven above us. But the sounds changed. Suddenly the player halted — the grand strains ceased, and there was substituted, with all its peculiar, touching beauty, "I know that my Redeemer liveth." I looked at my companion in some wonder, but we neither of us spoke. Suddenly I was tapped on the shoulder. To my great surprise it was the organist.

"Who is the player?" he asked.

"Dear me! I thought it was you."

"I had better go up and see," he said, and he ascended to the gallery. The music ceased as he started, and directly after I was called loudly. Both I and my companion ran up in haste. In the organist's arms was Miss Clara Leslie.

"She has fainted, I think," he said immediately. "We must get her into the open air." I took the fragile form from him, and bore it hastily into the churchyard. There, for the first time, I looked carefully at the face. I found that for any good the air could do, my burden might as well have remained in the organ gallery, for any harm that wind or cold could work it would matter nothing if it never left the tomb-stone on which I laid it. To play that organ had been a frequent amusement to that sweet girl when in health and strength; this evening she had somehow escaped the vigilance of those who nursed her, and sitting in the old place, and playing the old tune so dear to her recollection, she had glided from the world.

" There, sir," concluded Mr. Jones, displaying a degree of emotion downright discreditable to a Relieving Officer, and which ought to have been brought to the notice of the Board—" I have done."

The angel of death was very good, and we are only selfish who sorrow at his doing.

XVII.—DIED THROUGH STARVATION.

PART I.

On a dreary November day, said Mr. Jones, continuing his "Recollections," a poor young woman, in the last stage of illness, was brought to the workhouse. Who she was or where she came from could not in the least degree be ascertained, for she was speechless, and no name appeared on any of her clothing. She had been found lying by the road-side just out of the town, and a compassionate passer-by having procured assistance, at once conveyed her to the only place where a person in such wretched condition would be received. The doctor was soon in attendance.

"Not much to be done there," he said, shaking his head.

The master of the workhouse and I were standing by the bed-side.

"Poor thing!" I murmured, "is she actually dying? She can't be more than twenty."

"No, but worn out, nevertheless," was the reply. "It is not a usual case, I'm sure," continued the surgeon, scanning the poor pale face, and gently lifting the thin left hand.

The master nodded his head.

"That poor girl little thought, a year or two back, to come to that pass," he said. "She will die in a workhouse, but she was born in a very different place, that I'll pledge myself to."

I accquiesced. You may wonder, sir, at our thus so positively judging when we had such very slight foundation for an opinion. But just as the police have a marvellously quick eye for certain small outward differences between an honest man and a thief. so we, who see so much of poverty, can distinguish in a moment between persons who have been all their lives in a lowly condition, and such as have been reduced to indigence by untoward circumstances. This young woman was well born, and had been well cared for the greater part of her life; not the dreary condition in which she had been found, not her wan, wasted form and features, nor the soiled clothing which we had taken off her, misled us. We felt sure we were gazing upon one to whom comforts, nay, luxuries, had been familiar, as sure as that we now saw her on a workhouse bed, only a short time before we should have to commit her to a pauper's grave.

People say we New Poor Law Officials are not acquainted with such things as hearts, but it is not true. Doctors are not brutal because they do not cry over sick people, neither are we without compassion because we do not fondle poverty, or seek to soothe it with soft words. As we three men stood and looked at that forlorn being, so young, and with the remains of so much beauty and grace still manifest, we were greatly concerned, and very sorrowful.

The doctor essayed to give her a drop or two of brandy in a teaspoon.

"I do believe she is literally dying of starvation," he muttered, "yet she's past taking food."

A feeble movement of the lips ensued from the application of the stimulant, but there was no further sign of revival. As we could be of no use, we gave the poor creature in charge to a nurse, and left her.

I was quitting the workhouse when I was called back by the porter.

"Mr. Jones, we have found this brooch in the pocket of the young woman brought in just now. We had overlooked it."

He put the trinket in my hand. It was rather large, and of very peculiar shape, and contained a lock of light brown hair. On the back were the initials E. M., and a date. I told the man to hand it to the master. The words had scarcely passed my lips, when the nurse appeared.

"She is gone, sir," she said.

"Dead! what, so soon?" I exclaimed.

"She gave a sigh, sir, and it was all over. You know she was barely alive when you called me to her."

Under the circumstances, notice was given to the coroner, and an inquest was held, but nothing fresh was elicited. The examination of the body did not lead to any decisive results. The doctor could discover no trace of poison, and he believed the deceased had died from sheer inanition, but he was not sure. A verdict of "Died through starvation" was returned, and the subject dropped. The remains of the luckless girl were deposited in Bramblestone churchyard, and thus her brief history ended.

Several months afterwards, a discovery was made which ought to have been made long previously. I do not know how it chanced, but the girl's clothing had not been destroyed. One day an infirmary nurse said to me—

"Sir, I want to tell you that looking a little while back at this (holding up some under clothing), which belonged to that poor girl who was brought here dying some time back, I discovered this name written inside. I am very sorry, sir, I did not see it at the time."

"So am I, Mrs. Marks, it ought to have been communicated at the inquest. We shall be called to account for carelessness. Let me see the name."

She displayed it.

"Emmeline Waverley."

"Be particular to preserve that piece of clothing, Mrs. Marks."

"Yes, sir."

PART II.

THE host of "The Flying Eagle" stood outside his door one fine afternoon superintending the carriage into the inn of sundry large boxes, just arrived by railway. The branch line to Bramblestone had not long been opened, and its effect was beginning to manifest itself. This bright summer weather had brought many visitors to Bramblestone; the "Flying Eagle" was doing good business, and apartments were at high prices.

"Your friends, there, are not going away in a hurry," I jested, as I passed merry old John Banks. "Visitors for the whole season, I fancy."

"A rare lot of packages, truly," replied John, "but I don't know as to their stopping the season. There be two of them, Mr. Jones—man and wife. One of them, I think, won't leave us again, the other will leave us very quick."

As this not over-clear observation was delivered in a mysterious whisper, with a vast number of odd shakes of the head and shrugs of the shoulders, I naturally besought an explanation.

"The poor lady will find lodgings in the bigger inn than mine, yonder," responded John, in an undertone, "where there's one charge once for all, and plenty of room, and beds are always ready."

I guessed his meaning.

"The church-yard, eh, John?"

"Aye, aye, Mr. Jones; we shall keep her with us. Poor thing! A thorough brute!"

"She's a poor thing, and he's a thorough brute," explained John, in reply to my look of surprise. "My belief is, sir, he's killing her," he whispered; "I should like to——" and John performed a movement as though he had a fated fowl in his grasp. "They're coming out," he said hastily.

A lady and gentleman issued from the inn door. The lady was evidently very ill, and leant heavily on the gentleman's arm.

"How we can have come to a place like this," growled the gentleman; "how we can have been such idiots, really——"

"Never mind," urged the lady; "it is a beautiful spot, and——"

"Drat you!" roared her companion at one of the porters; "if you upset that parcel your master shall pay me fifty pounds."

"Begging your pardon, no, sir," interposed John, with a ruffled air. "I won't be answerable for any things of that value, and the man is taking every care."

The gentleman surveyed honest John as though he would strike him down, but he said nothing, and passed on with his companion.

"Who are they?" I asked of John.

"The name of Waverley is on the trunks," he replied.

Waverley! I thought I had some reason for remembering the name. After the usual hunting in odd corners of recollection which follow upon the attempting to satisfy a vague fancy, I lighted upon an explanation. It was the name which the workhouse nurse had discovered on the under clothing of the unfortunate girl who had been brought into the infirmary, three or four years back, only to die there. It was a very uncommon name, and I determined at once to learn from the parties themselves whether they had had any relationship with the dead girl.

The visitors soon reappeared. While I stood talking to John they came back, the gentleman still grumbling, the lady drooping and silent.

Outside the "Flying Eagle" was a magnificent old tree, under which were placed some garden chairs. The lady cast her eyes on these.

"Sit you down on one of these chairs, Emmeline," said the gentleman, "as you find you are not able to move at my pace; you'll get the air there, and meantime I'll try and bring back the life into me, which always dies out when I go creeping about with you."

Without noticing this considerate remark, the lady sunk into one of the chairs, and in a minute the gentleman was almost out of sight.

I have thought since that I ought to have reflected before taking the course I then, on the impulse of the moment, at once pursued. But the opportunity was tempting for making an enquiry of the lady, which, in any case, I felt sure would be civilly answered, in preference to questioning the gentleman, who, I was equally sure, would, in any case, be exceedingly rude.

John had moved away, and there was no one by. I advanced, and bowing, said:

"Madame, my name is Jones. I am the Relieving Officer of this Union. Would you permit me to make an enquiry of you?"

She looked much surprised, but courteously bent her head.

"A few years back," I continued, "a poor girl, some twenty years of age, was discovered at the point of death in a lane near here. She was brought to the workhouse; she died within an hour, and lies buried in our churchyard. At first no name was perceived on her clothing, but there was found upon her a brooch, which is still at the workhouse, and which I will describe to you."

I described it minutely. As I proceeded the lady rose from her seat, an expression of wild horror settled in her eyes, and she gasped for breath. I saw a very painful discovery at hand, and I was half sorry I had ventured the enquiry; but it was too late to draw back.

"I know it, I know it," she tremulously whispered; "tell me."

"I greatly fear," I said, "I am causing pain, but your name struck on my recollection, and——"

"But you said you had not learnt the name of my— my——"

"Some time afterwards," I gently interrupted, "a name *was* discovered on the clothing, and——"

"Don't tell me," almost shrieked the invalid, and the next instant, still more wildly, she exclaimed, "Yes, yes—say, say—the name was——"

"Emmeline Waverley."

"I thought so," was faintly murmured, and the lady fell back senseless.

She was conveyed into the house and to bed. I heard afterwards that when Mr. Waverley returned she was delirious, but in her delirium she repeated almost precisely the conversation which had ensued between us.

Late in the evening I was sauntering a little way out of Bramblestone, when I saw Mr. Waverley coming towards me. I knew him directly. He looked hard at me, and stopped. I then saw he was slightly intoxicated.

"In this hole of a place one can scarcely make mistakes," he said; "you must be the Relieving Officer. They said you had come this way."

"You are right," I replied, quietly; "what do you want of me?"

"I want nothing of you," he said insultingly, "except not to meddle with me and mine; not to go talking of things or to people without cause. If I had been by this afternoon when you began chattering to my wife, I would have prevented you repeating it one while, Mr. Relieving Officer, let me tell you that."

"I have not talked of things or to people without cause," I answered. "The inquiry of Mrs. Waverley was suggested by my duty, and——"

"Look you, and don't talk. Hang your duty: you country fellows haven't wit enough to talk. Now hear me talk, and don't interrupt me—attend. Say not a word to anybody about what passed between you and Mrs. Waverley to-day. You have made her very ill. That's enough. Keep your tongue silent, and here's a sovereign for you."

I could scarcely help laughing; the bribe was offered with an air befitting the bestowal of an irresistible benefit, and when the briber found no hand stretched forth to receive his princely gift, he staggered back in astonishment and anger.

"Put your money in your pocket, sir," I said sternly; "and before you exclaim against the nonsense of other people, set a guard over your own lips. My duty in this matter is very simple. You have gathered, apparently, the substance of my conversation with Mrs. Waverley this morning. I put to you the question which I should have put to her. Can you tell me anything of Emmeline Waverley, who died in our workhouse two or three years back?"

The answer I expected came. He struck straight at me; I avoided the blow, and he fell. Before he had recovered himself I was several yards off, and he did not follow me.

I was determined to unveil the mystery of the evident relationship between these people and that hapless girl. I continued my walk till quite a late hour, pondering my next step to that end. It was perfectly dark when I returned to Bramblestone. On my way home I was passing through our old churchyard; by day or night I always bring that churchyard into my journey if I can. The view from the place, as you know, sir, is beautiful. On a fine moonlight night it is a real treat to lean against the wall and gaze down into the rich valley beneath, and I never feel alone there; so many of my old friends and companions lie around, that I have a strange feeling of being only one of a pleasant party. I look about, and seem to wonder that I hear no voices; and then the voices come, men's voices, strong and hearty, soft tones of women's, and little children's shrill utterances I hear in every direction. But I am forgetting my story; even a Relieving Officer, you see, sir, verges on the sentimental at times.

A scream—another, and another—from a remote corner of the churchyard; I leapt over (without noise) the intervening graves, and saw a woman struggling with a man. And then I slunk back and hid behind a tombstone, for by the moonlight I perceived the woman to be the strange lady at the inn, and the man to be the brute, her husband.

"Let me go," exclaimed the former, "or I will rouse the neighbourhood!"

"I'll strangle you first!" was the reply.

The screams again rose, then fell, then were heard afresh, but weaker. I sprung forward, and wrested the poor woman from the scoundrel's grasp. The next moment I received a blow which dashed me against a gravestone, and made me sick and giddy. The scream now sounded piercingly, and help came. Two men, who were passing, scrambled to the spot. At sight of them my aggressor tried to hide himself, not that he would have done himself much service if he had been successful, but he acted on the momentary impulse. The men saw him, and dashed after him. He rushed on heedlessly, struck his foot against a low stone, fell forward with terrific force against a high one, rolled over and over a level space, and then lay perfectly still. I had recovered, and hastened to the spot, leaving the lady in a faint.

"What, you here, Mr. Jones!" cried one of the men, recognising me.

"Yes, don't ask any questions now. Is the gentleman much hurt?"

We all three bent over him, and then stared in each other's faces aghast. We said nothing for a moment, then I directed.

"Take him to the Flying Eagle. Say I shall be there immediately."

The men shouldered their burden. They had scarcely done so, when a whole heap of people crowded into the churchyard. At their head was the landlord of the inn just named. He was in a great state of excitement.

"Have you found the lady?" he cried. "Bless my heart now, have you found the lady? Oh, it's you, Mr. Jones—do tell me, have you found the lady? The carelessness of that girl Mary, to go and leave an invalid not quite right in her mind, and let her escape out of the window. Dear! dear! dear! now have you found the lady?"

This explained the mystery. Poor Mrs. Waverley had been left to herself, and the statement I had made to her of that poor girl being buried in our churchyard, still weighing upon her in her delirious condition, she had escaped out of the bedroom window (which she could easily accomplish at the Flying Eagle) and had found her way thither. How her husband had discovered her in the churchyard, I never heard. John and his people had been busy searching in the neighbourhood for the runaway, when her screams attracted them to the right quarter.

"The lady is in that corner," I replied hurriedly to John's enquiry. "They had better carry her carefully to the inn through the west gate. This is Mr. Waverley, who has hurt himself; we will bring him to the inn through the south gate. Don't say anything to Mrs. Waverley about the accident to her husband."

He was dead. I felt sure he was dead, even from the momentary examination. Here was a fresh tragic incident! What miserable fatality attached to these Waverleys! There was the poor girl in her grave, who, I was satisfied, had been some near relative. There was Mrs. Waverley at death's door, in a decline, and now her monster of a husband lay a corpse, through an accident. Unfortunate family—under how dark a shadow had it rested!

For days Mrs. Waverley lay at the inn, dangerously ill. The residence of some of her relatives having been ascertained, a communication was forwarded, which quickly brought them to her bedside. They took charge of her, and at the proper time revealed to her her husband's fate. She was too ill now to be removed. John's prophecy would prove true.

I was summoned one afternoon to see her. When I arrived, I found the relatives evidently wondering, but they asked no questions. I was admitted at once to the invalid's bedroom. She was quite alone. She lay on a couch before the window, which was open, for the weather was very warm.

"You are the gentleman who spoke to me when— you recollect," she said very faintly, but pleasingly; "I want you to show me—that brooch. I am very ill. You will oblige me."

I had guessed her purpose in sending for me, and I had brought the ornament.

"I anticipated your wish." And I gave it her.

She held it lovingly in her hand—turned it round and round, kissed it, and then returned it to me.

"I will leave it with you."

"No; but if you do not need to keep it, I will tell you what to do with it."

"I will readily comply with any wish you may express regarding it."

"They will lay me there," she murmured, bending her head in the direction of the churchyard. "They have promised me. Will you attend my funeral, and when nobody is by, drop it in my grave?"

"Certainly."

"I may trust you," she said abruptly, scanning my face. "Promise me something else."

I waited.

"You have children ?"

"I have one daughter."

"Protect her, in God's name. I *had* a daughter. Her name was—"

I heard no sound, but I guessed her revelation. The daughter's name had been "Emmeline."

The mourners had left the grave side.   I advanced.

"What was that fell upon the coffin?" asked the grave-digger.   "Did you drop anything, sir?"

I did not answer, but with my foot moved some earth into the grave.

"Close it up, Williams—it's the bed we shall all occupy."

With an "aye, aye, sir, that's true, sure enough," he shovelled in the earth, and the brooch rested undisturbed upon the coffin.

Circumstances which afterwards became known, explained to a great extent the fate of Emmeline Waverley. Her mother, a widow, married Mr. Waverley, her cousin. Alas, for her! a base and unspeakably bad man he was. His wife was in possession of a considerable sum of money settled upon her by her father.   She was in bad health, and openly intimated her intention of bequeathing this property to her daughter Emmeline; so Mr. Waverley determined that this incubus should be got rid of.   The precise details of the mode in which he accomplished his object, I never heard, but I believe he worked in two ways.   The girl was vain and hot-tempered; he treated her with indignity.   She was handsome and thoughtless; he actually schemed for her the worst temptations.

He succeeded.   The death-bed scene in Bramblestone workhouse showed that he had succeeded.   That is all I know; but one circumstance more I may mention, because it is a strange and stirring circumstance, and I

never think of it without a thrill. You remember, sir,
that the body of Mr. Waverley, after he had received
the blow which caused his death, rolled, as I described
to you, over a level space, and then rested. Over what
level space do you think it rolled, and where do you
think it rested? It rolled over the little boundary which
marked the union burial-ground, and it rested on the
grave of the unfortunate Emmeline. There is retribution, sometimes, even in this world.

XVIII.—MR. FLACK'S MARRIAGE.
PART I.

THE people of this world are very selfish; the Bramblestonians were no exception to the rule. When they
heard John Toplis, of Sunny Farm, was dead, they sor-
rowed, for Toplis was a right useful man in the place,
always ready to help a neighbour in difficulty, with
labour, and with money too, so far as his limited means
would allow, and his death, therefore, was a real loss.
They wished it had been Anne Toplis, his wife, who had
not shared her late husband's liberal disposition, and
whose absence would have been no cause for weeping.
And when Minnie Toplis died a few days after her
father—Minnie, a sweet, much-loved girl of eighteen—
the mother still being left, the Bramblestonians were
downright angry. The only members of the family they
regarded—and these regarded so sincerely—both gone

for aye, the hard and sullen woman remaining, from whom, was roundly asserted, no good ever came, or would come. But the Bramblestonians were wrong in this. Good did come from Anne Toplis at a later day, and my story is anent thereto.

Typhus fever was the malady which carried off poor John Toplis and his daughter. Nothwithstanding their regard for the sufferers, the country people kept clear of the cottage wherein they lay; but a numerous body followed the coffins to the grave. No sympathy was extended to the widow. She looked about for some, but only met cold and churlish glances. She understood them. The Bramblestonians might as well have said openly, "We wish you were where they lie, and that they had been spared." Those words were written in their faces, and Anne Toplis read them. It was enough. She withdrew her eyes. She would not afterwards have received any condolences, had they been offered. She was never friendly with the people around her. She hated them now. She and the Bramblestonians would never exchange an unnecessary word.

And through long years did that lone woman live at the Sunny Farm House (the land was let), going abroad only about once a week, and never, by any chance, admitting any one within its doors. She must have been ill sometimes, but no doctor ever went. At church she never was seen. The food she purchased was so inferior in quality, and so scant in quantity, that the tradesmen were aghast. By and by, her appearance

used to excite positive awe. The boys no longer laughed
and jeered; they shrunk away in fear. They would
not have met her out of the town alone for a half-holi-
day and a plum cake. In former times Anne Toplis
would have been in sore danger of a witch's doom. Not
that she was ever known to hurt anybody. No matter,
however, for that; she was old, ill-favoured, silent,
and had an air of mystery about her. Enough. The
sagacious and benevolent people of an age gone-by
would have detected at once the witch malignity, and
Anne Toplis would soon have suffered the witch's fate.

But as the pleasant spectacle of a bonfire, with Anne
Toplis seated upon it, could not be realised in this later
day, the good people of Bramblestone could do nought
but marvel and sorrow at their want of power to bring
this fear-exciting woman to account. The butcher and
baker both agreed not to serve her; yet, when afterwards she walked quietly into their shops as usual, and
made her small requirements, they *did* serve her, so that
scheme fell through. Then it was reported that the
widow did not live alone in the farm house, but that
some one was with her; and one bold man declared he
would get sight of the interior of the house, and learn
the truth of the rumour. "I'll have a peep at it, if I die
for it," he said; and he was the pig-killer of Bramblestone, a man so hardened by a long and extensive practice of his profession, that, armed with the dreadful
weapon which had carried death into so many of the
porcine race, there is nothing, I do believe, he would

not have dared or done, if need be—so it was quite certain he would make the attempt. Well, it was made. He called at Sunny Farm House late one night, upon some pretext, and when he reached home, he told his wife he had been half over the house, that he had seen most awful things, and she should have the whole story in the morning. But the morning in this world, to the pig-killer, never came: he died in his sleep. And when the gossips of Bramblestone heard the circumstances, they quaked with most profound horror. No one sought to play tricks in any way with Anne Toplis after this dismal event. The butcher would rather have even given her his prime joints than have quarrelled with her; the baker would sooner have pressed her acceptance of hot rolls and milk loaves daily, than have been visited by a frown.

And yet, as you will suppose, the mystery about Anne Toplis might soon have been penetrated. She was a peculiar, but not a remarkable woman. Being ill-treated by the Bramblestonians, she disliked and avoided them, and the more they kept away from her, the more she shunned them. For her miserable mode of living a cause was not by any means apparent. It was known that Toplis had left property behind him—not much, perhaps, but sufficient to enable her to live in fair comfort. A reason, however, for Anne Toplis's self-torture by means of gradual starvation, of course there was. She had become a miser, and gloated over her savings. She had no heaps of sovereigns in her house; her delight was not that insane pleasure felt in handling gold and hiding it in a secure place. Anne Toplis simply accumulated money. She spent not a farthing unnecessarily, and not a pound did she allow to lie idle. She was, as a miser, very wise and shrewd, was that most foolish and obtuse woman.

On a November night, foggy and drear, a man was trudging homeward past Sunny Farm. The unusual sight of a light in one of the rooms of the farm house attracted his attention. Though a mizzling rain was falling, and the cold and wet together were powerful stimulants to get within doors as soon as possible, the man was induced to stop for a moment and contemplate the light. As he did so, a loud scream and cry for help issued from the house. He was but of diminutive stature was the traveller, and the slight hesitation which he at first manifested was quite excusable; but in another minute he had entered the house (the door being unfastened), and was in the room whence came the light. The moment of his entrance was the moment of another man's exit. Straight away, almost head over heels, downstairs, into the road, and off as fast as his legs could carry him, dashed a burglar, certainly not one of the bravest of his class. On the floor, panting and exhausted, lay Anne Toplis.

With something, it must be owned, of an inward tremor, the stranger lifted the prostrate form on to a bed.

"Is the villian gone?" enquired Anne, hoarsely.

"Yes, he's far enough off by this time, I take it,"

was answered cheerfully. "You should have some one to stay with you, Mrs. Toplis. This house is too lonely for you to live in it by yourself."

"Oh—you are—yes, I see," said the widow, rousing herself, and looking the speaker full in the face. "Well, I'm glad you helped me instead of anyone else. John used to like you, and you were never uncivil to me, as almost every soul of the crew yonder has been at some time or other."

"Nonsense, Mrs. Toplis, that's all your fancy. If you will shun the townspeople, and live so solitary as you do, how can you wonder at the separation which exists between you. Now let me persuade you. Give me leave to say you will be glad to see some of them here to-morrow—yes, say to-morrow."

"I'd rather there came fifty robbers than one of those hateful Bramblestone people," was the passionate reply. "You saved me to-night, and I am obliged to you. Now do me a further favour. Don't say to a single person that you have been in here. It will be for your good not to do so."

"I will not," answered the young man (he was not eight-and-twenty), rather recoiling, as an ominous recollection of the pig-killer's fate crossed him.

"Say not a syllable about what has occurred," continued the widow. "I should have the place beset to-morrow by idiots of busy-bodies. You may come again, if you like. I am in your debt for to-night's service, but not another creature shall enter here while Annie Toplis lives. Good night."

The young man, half sorrowful, half angry, bade the
strange woman good evening, and departed. When he
had left the gate he could not help looking back at the
house, pondering the peculiar morbid feeling which
could induce any one to live the life of widow Toplis.
"I suppose there's some pleasure in existence," he
thought, "even under such circumstances as those.
For myself, I'd sooner be—yes, I'd sooner be, indeed I
would—in the workhouse." And half scared at the
idea of utter desolation which this preference indicated,
the Bramblestonian hastened his pace, and was soon in
his house and in bed. And in the dead of the night he
was visited by an awful vision of the pig-killer, who
surveying him much as he used to contemplate a choice
animal on which he was about to exercise his skill,
caused the horified sleeper to shriek with horror and
yell for mercy which was denied, for the pig-killer
smilingly raised the dreadful knife, then plunged it with
all his force into the body of his wretched victim—and
woke him.

PART II.

"Do you think, sir, if I was to get married, the Guardians would raise my salary?"

Such was the question put to me one morning by my
assistant, Mr. Flack.

I regarded my rather youthful fellow-labourer with
smiling astonishment. Married, indeed! The Guardians were not likely to help him to a course which, in

all probability, would by and by add to the parish burdens.

"Upon my word, Mr. Flack, I am very dubious on the point. My impression inclines, however, in the unfavourable direction."

Mr. Flack looked dismal.

"Why, this is something new," I remarked. "When did your views turn towards matrimony?"

"Well, it's no secret," answered the little man, cheering up, (it was impossible for him to be downcast more than a minute). "I was introduced last night to Seraphina Miskin. It was a tea-party at Farmer Goodland's."

"But do I understand that you had never seen the young lady before?" I asked, rather surprised at the expedition with which a climax had been reached.

"Never! never!" replied my small assistant, with a theatrical air. "She came into the room at seven o'clock—at five minutes past I was greatly interested in her; at half-past I was powerfully excited; at eight I declared myself, offered my heart, my mind, my body, my—my—"

"Yes, I know—your everything, in short. Well, and—"

"At five minutes past eight I was—"

"Bravo!—accepted."

"No, not bravo—I was refused," said poor Mr. Flack, his colour fading, and with despair in his countenance.

"But she *would* have had me," cried the little man,

again brightening up, "only, alas! she has a hard-hearted father, and I have a villanous rival."

"Who is he ?"

Flack ground his teeth—"Smirks."

"What! young Smirks down at Wry-neck Farm ? He's no great catch for a smart girl. Why, he's only one eye."

"No, but he's five hundred pounds."

"He limps shockingly. You may say he has but one leg."

"No, but he's five hundred pounds."

"Then, he's only a degree or two above an idiot. He hasn't an idea in his head."

"No, but he's five hundred pounds in his pocket," again moaned poor Flack.

"But bless me, Flack," said I, becoming interested, "the five hundred pounds won't cover all these defects. Why, what does Miss Seraphina say ?"

"She hates him," answered the distressed lover vehemently. "She says she'll poison herself rather than marry him. She asked my advice as to the best kind of poison, and the cheapest shop at which to buy it."

All this was vastly absurd, of course, yet I could not help feeling sorry for the little man. An upright, hard-working, intelligent assistant was Flack. This was the first time he had fallen in love, and he had tumbled in so instantaneously and so completely, that he was slightly crazed. He could talk of nothing else, and in the course of a day or two he became so disturbed men-

tally, that I was quite sorry, and scarcely knew what
to do with him. He had just left me, looking exceedingly like a man bidding for a strait waistcoat, his
face flushed, and his eyes glistening, when the Vestry
Clerk of Bramblestone, Mr. Moneyworth, came up to
me. He was a very pleasant, good-hearted man.

"What's the matter with your little fellow, yonder?"
he asked, nodding in the direction in which Flack had
gone.

I told him the story, in confidence. He laughed.

"I like Flack," he said, "always have liked him.
Now tell me, do you know this girl?"

"Yes, she's all very well—Flack might do worse.
But I can quite understand what he says about her
father. The old man thinks of nothing but money;
and as Smirk has, I imagine, rather a better income than
Flack, and this lump sum of five hundred pounds,
whereas Flack has nothing, Smirk will be the man, if
it remains with the father, depend upon it."

"Humph! well, I don't know—but I must be off.
You know that poor old woman Toplis is gone, I suppose."

"Dear me! no."

"Died a few hours ago. I was there at the time."

"You!"

"Yes, she sent for me to make her will. Had such
a horror of her, that I almost doubted whether I would
go, but obeyed duty. Was very glad I went. Uncommonly good will. Left a tidy little sum behind

her, more than people will expect. One way and
another, there's fully a thousand pounds."

"Dear me! and as the poor old woman is now dead,
may I ask what she's done with her money?"

"Yes, it will soon be no secret. Smirks will know
all about it soon."

"Smirks! Why, now, Mr. Moneyworth, you don't
surely mean to say Anne Toplis made a good will,
when she left her money to Smirks, either father or
son."

"I didn't say she'd left it to either of the Smirks.
You are too fast, Mr. Jones. I only said Smirks would
soon know all about the will. No, the old lady showed
at the last she had, at all events, one good quality—
gratitude."

"Then the property's gone out of Bramblestone,
that's certain; for to not a human being in this place
did Anne Toplis owe anything like gratitude, I fancy."

"There you're wrong, now. One person, whom you
well know, had visited her, attended to her wants,
comforted her, and finally held her hand when death
grasped her. Have you any idea who I mean?"

"Not the smallest."

"I thought not, I thought he had kept his promise·
The person was yonder poor lover, Flack."

"Flack! bless me. I never heard a word of it, he
never told me."

"No. I heard the whole, story from him, after her
death. He had saved her from robbery, perhaps mur-

der, one night, some months back. Never mind the
details now. She made him promise not to mention
the circumstances to any one, but he might, if he liked,
come to her again himself. He went several times,
his attention pleased her, and the result has been she
has left him all her money."

"I'm right glad to hear it. Here, let me send for
him. I suppose he may know at once his good fortune."

"Never mind at the moment; I will formally communicate it to him. I have not opened the will yet.
I'll go and do it at once, good-bye."

He had scarcely gone when Flack re-appeared.

"Flack," I said, "you did not tell me of Anne Toplis's death."

"I really forgot, sir," he replied. "Yes, poor thing,
she died this morning."

"And I was quite ignorant, too, that you, out of all
the Bramblestone people, had alone been admitted to
her house, and been friendly with her for months past."

"Mr. Moneyworth has told you, I suppose. Yes,
poor old woman, I was of some little use to her towards
the last; and very glad I was to be so."

"Now, Frank Flack," I said, taking him in friendly
fashion by the shoulders, "you're an honest fellow,
Frank Flack—tell me if you knew what would come of
this?"

He turned pale. "There was nothing wrong in it,
sir. I couldn't mention it, because she told me not.

Poor old woman, I grew quite to like her at last. But
why do you look at me so oddly ?"

" Do you know she made a will, Flack ?"

" Yes, that I do know, because, by her desire, I fetched
Mr. Moneyworth."

"I suppose it never by any chance suggested itself
to you, that you might benefit by this will."

"I certainly have thought the old lady may have
left me a suit of mourning."

" Well, I believe I may tell you she has done so."

"And very kind of her," answered the unsophisti-
cated Assistant Relieving Officer. "All I did for her
amounted to nothing."

A few days gone by, behold my worthy assistant
with a countenance as buoyant as it had before been
downcast.

" Well, Flack," I said, " all arranged, I suppose. Is
the day fixed ?"

"Yes, sir; all straight now. Tuesday week is the
day; delays, you know, are dangerous."

" Well, upon my word, that motto seems to stimulate
you. The falling in love, the proposal, the marriage,
all within three weeks! That is railroad pace indeed!
But what has become of young Smirks? Does not your
conscience smite you for the injury you've done that
unfortunate young man ?"

" Oh, he's not unfortunate, sir, he's all right; he's coming to the wedding."

" To the wedding !"

" Yes. In fact, he has some idea of being married on the same day."

" Married ! Same day ! bless me, what do you mean ?"

" O, you hav'n't heard then ! Why, no sooner did Smirk find himself put aside by Seraphina Miskin, than he offered himself to Amelia Maples, and was accepted, of course."

" Accepted, of course ! And by a nice comely girl like Amelia Maples ! Well, I cannot think what has come over the Bramblestone girls. The idea of Amelia Maples, good-looking, sprightly, intelligent, going to marry the lame, one-eyed, half-foolish, Sam Smirks !"

" Well, sir, it is odd, but then you know——"

" Ah, I guess what you are about to say, but it's all nothing, Flack, it's absolutely nothing."

" Yes, sir, it is something. It's a great deal. It's—five hundred pounds !"

XIX.—A RELIEVING OFFICER'S DANGERS.

" The occupation of a Relieving Officer is never particularly exhilarating," said Mr. Jones to me one day,
" and occasionally it is exceedingly disagreeable. It is
even dangerous now and then. As I have often observed to you when we have been chatting, paupers
never exhibit anything like gratitude; application is
probably not made to the union except under the pressure of absolute necessity, and then the feeling with
which, in nine cases out of ten, relief is asked is, that it
would certainly be denied, if the law did not compel its
bestowal. Then there is a fruitful source of irritation
in the mode of relief. For various reasons, the Guardians
may sometimes positively refuse out-door relief, while
the applicant may as positively reject the workhouse.
Again, an order may issue for the out-door relief in a
particular case to be wholly or partially in ' kind,' i.e.
in bread, whereas the applicant may prefer money. The
Reliving Officer, of course, as the adviser of the Board,
comes in for heaps of ill-will, be he as attentive and
considerate as he may. Sometimes this ill-will finds
vent even in personal violence; I am very thankful I
am standing talking to you now alive and well. It was
not the fault of a certain Joe Markles, a pauper of

former days, that I was not laid in my grave with a bullet through my brain.

"A few years make all the difference, sir, at my time of life. When Joe Markles one day so pestered and worried, annoyed and insulted me, that I lost all patience, I being then a very strong man, took him by the shoulders and put him out of the union office. When I had done it I was sorry, I had lost myself somewhat. A Relieving Officer ought always to command his temper, and mine had mastered me; however, the deed could not be undone. There the man was outside, using the most horrible language, and threatening me in most bloodthirsty fashion. After awhile he went away, and his first visit was to the Guardian of the parish to which he belonged, to whom he made a complaint so absurdly exaggerated, that the Guardian would not entertain it. Afterwards he wrote to the Board of Guardians, and due enquiry having been made, the result was again unsatisfactory to the complainant. Lastly, he addressed the Poor Law Commissioners, who communicated with the Board, and received in reply a statement of the facts which led to his complaint to them also being summarily dismissed. Then Joe Markles grew savage and desperate, and swore he would not be disappointed of paying me out somehow, and that the first opportunity he would murder me.

"I remember my wife was in a great fidget and alarm when she heard of this formidable threat, and

coupled it with the sanguinary character of the man.
I was about in all hours, and there was not the slightest
difficulty in the way of Joe's kind intention being carried out any day he pleased. I deemed it best not to
lodge any information against the man, it would only
aggravate him further, so I determined to brave the unpleasant contingency of becoming his victim. I suppose
if a Relieving Officer were to say he could dare an as-
sassin in the performance of his duty, he would be
laughed at. Heroism in a Relieving Officer! What
next?

"Although Markles' complaint of assault against me
was dismissed, his application for relief was granted.
There was no doubt he was in distress; for after being
absent from Bramblestone some time, he had had no
ostensible work since his return, his newly-married
wife was ailing, and Joe belonged to no friendly club.
But here arose a dissension over the form of relief. Joe
had a character for the reverse of sobriety, and the
Guardians would only trust him with a mere trifle in
money, while they awarded him and his wife a liberal
weekly allowance of bread. This did not suit Joe at all,
and his animosity against me (for to my debit be placed
the unpalatable order) had now arrived at boiling pitch.

"The day after this decision of the Board I paid a
visit, as was my duty, to Joe's house. I do believe the
tears were in my wife's eyes as I said good-bye to her
before starting. She evidently had the most terrible
misgivings, and I was obliged to hurry off to avoid a

R

scene with her. I, myself, heartily wished Markles out of the neighbourhood; but while he was in it I must do the best I could with him, and bear all consequences.

"I was curious to see Markles' wife, or the woman who passed for his wife. He had only a few months before brought her to Bramblestone, and I had been told she had come from a far-off village, where were relatives very near and dear to me; but as it happened, I had never met her. I had already written, making some enquiries, but had not yet received an answer.

"I was not sorry to find, when I reached the cottage, which was fully a mile from Bramblestone, that the respected Joe was not within; and his wife, or reputed wife, might have been from home too, for anything I could make out of her. Whether even the pittance of money which had been received that day had been expended in ardent spirit, or the bread had been bartered in exchange for the pernicious liquid, I could not discover, but the condition of Mrs. Markles was in the last degree unsatisfactory.

"I was exasperated.

"'So this is the use to which you apply the very first money you get from the Guardians!' I exclaimed, exhibiting to view a suspiciously-shaped green bottle, from which proceeded an odour unfortunately beyond suspicion. 'I'll stop this, Mrs. Markles, you may rely upon it.'

"'Stop—what—eh—Mr.—what is it—dunt know—I say, there, now—dunt know—what you mean?'"

"'I say you're drunk, Mrs. Markles, and very sorry I am to say it.'

"At this preposterous assertion of mine the good lady set up a perfect shriek of laughter.

"I turned to go.

"'I say,' she said, taking me affectionately by the arm, 'wait a few minutes—now, do; *Joe 'll be here directly.*'

"'I'm in a hurry,' I replied, certainly not less disposed to depart by the announcement just made, and I released my arm and returned to Bramblestone with speed a little more than ordinary.

"It was the day before next Board day. In the morning I had received a letter from one of the relatives to whom I had written inquiring about Mrs. Markles. The contents of this letter were unexpected, and interested me. Sarah Tavin had been well known to my relatives. They (two dear, kind old ladies) had befriended her from childhood, and she, for some time, had lived with them as servant. Then Joe Markles made his appearance on the scene, and there was but one part which he could play or did play anywhere, and it was that of an unmitigated scoundrel. He performed it to perfection in the village of Strangleys. But only in one quarter did he gain approval — that quarter was the luckless girl Sarah Tavin. For months previously Sarah had been rather losing credit, much to the sorrow of her friends. Now it was as though she scraped together all she had left, and by one act demolished it. She married

Joe Markles, and with him left the village, and came to Bramblestone.

"I knew pretty well her history subsequently, and what a life she had suffered with Markles. I could have pitied her, but that from all accounts the effect of the penalty of her folly had not been to impress and humble, but to harden her and deepen her degradation. She had come to imitate her husband's depravities, and follow him in his abominable courses. I saw only one termination to their career—the blackest ruin.

"On the next day I was bound to report to the Board the state in which I had found the abandoned woman on the occasion of my visit. Of course, all relief would be withdrawn, and then I felt sure that some catastrophe would ensue. Pained at this conviction, I determined to make a second visit to the cottage.

"I confess I felt a strange reluctance to go. Perhaps I could not quite cast out of my thoughts a report made to me that Markles, looking more ferocious and desperate than ever, had been seen hovering about my house several times during the morning. He had been away for four or five days, and his re-appearance had attracted attention. A man of his stamp is a truly dangerous character. What feeling is there left in him giving you any hold upon him? He has no dread of punishment—he would rather escape it—but it does not weigh upon and control him. He is so thoroughly hardened, that the law has no terrors for him, The gallows is a thing to be cheated, certainly; but if the

cheat should fail, there will be no wincing or moaning
The cards have gone wrong, the penalty must be paid.
and here *is* the penalty. 'Say no more about it.'

"It was early in a November afternoon that I departed for the cottage. All our summer visitors had
disappeared, and the houses just outside Bramblestone
looked, if I may so speak, like corpses. Beyond them
stretched a wide common, rising into rather a high hill,
dividing Bramblestone from a deep valley on the other
side. At the bottom of this valley was Markles' cottage, and a wretched place it was. It contained only
two rooms, although they were of larger dimensions
than you would have expected. The bit of garden,
being utterly untended, was a mass of weeds, and a
heap of refuse was piled up actually by the cottage
door. The gate, being broken from its hinges, lay on
the ground, and of the garden railing scarce a fragment
remained.

"As I stood at the top of the hill looking down on
this deplorable dwelling, I felt such a presentiment of
evil about to happen to me, that I confess I hesitated,
and was half inclined to turn back. Why should I, an
humble Relieving Officer, dare a great peril without
anything approaching an equivalent? This villain was
not unlikely quietly waiting for me in yonder hovel,
and if I persevered, ere ten minutes should be past
I might be dying in agony on this very sward. But nonsense, Mr. Jones, it's your duty to proceed. I felt the
answer to be convincing—I must go—and I went.

" As I journeyed down the hill, I felt my coat tails pulled. I gave a most prodigious start, my heart almost leaped out of me. Turning round, I found a little child grasping me vigorously. He was about four years old, and such an object ! scarce a rag had he upon him, and so dirty was he, that his features were scarcely distinguishable.

" 'Please, you are to come to Mrs. Markles,' squeaked this pitiable morsel of humanity.

" ' I am coming now,' I replied; ' were you sent to fetch me, and who are you ?'

" ' Mrs. Markles told me to come, and I'm her servant.'

" I stared for a moment at the diminutive groom, and then inquired—

" ' What does Mrs. Markles want ?'

" ' She's dying, and wants brandy and prayers.'

" I formed an easy inference from this most singular and suggestive answer. Quickly I was at the cottage. The door was open. On entering, I saw Mrs. Markles lying on two chairs. Contrary to my expectations, she was not intoxicated, and really looked very ill, though not actually in a dying state. I judged her to be, as the saying is, ' not long for this world,' yet not one whit subdued was that quickly fallen and depraved woman. I could scarcely credit my relative's statement, that a year since she had been a well-conducted, fairly-principled person. There she lay now, with death no great way off, a hardened, despairing creature ;

her every look revealed her shocking state, hoping for, fearing nothing, here or hereafter.

"The aspect of Sarah Markles having thus impressed me, it may be imagined how her first words startled me.

"'Mr. Jones, I am very much obliged to you for coming,' she said, in a low voice, 'you will not be long troubled with me; I should like you to talk to me a little before I die. I feel my coffin is being made for me. Short, short time for repentance, Mr. Jones, but at least let me make the most of it.'

"Was she acting? I looked at and distrusted her. No godly sorrow was in her face, no moisture of dawning conversion in her eye.

"'I am exceedingly sorry to find you so ill. Let me go back and fetch the doctor to you.'

"'No, I would rather you stayed with me a bit. You must often be at the bedside of dying people, Mr. Jones. Find some words of comfort for me. There is little I can think of to cheer me for my long journey.'

"'Words of comfort,' I replied, 'there are which come naturally to the lips of every one. Repentance, perfect and sincere, can never be unavailing, Mrs. Markles. Forgiveness is always within reach, if we will but desire and seek it.'

"'I do desire and I do seek it, Mr. Jones.'

"'I am sincerely glad to hear it, and——'

"Never, so long as I live, shall I forget the thrill which ran through me. At the end of the room, which, as I have said, was of dimensions rather peculiarly large for a cottage in itself so small, a long, wide cloth hung across a high rail, stretching from wall to wall, so as to part off a few feet of the apartment from the remainder. In the centre of this cloth was a small hole, and my eye happening, while I spoke to rest attentively on this hole, another eye looking through from the other side became distinctly visible.

" 'And my fervent prayers shall be offered for you, Mrs. Markles.'

"The effort it cost me to complete the sentence I cannot describe, yet I hardly hesitated an instant, although the startling discovery I had made satisfied me my life was not worth five minutes' purchase : it was so utterly essential to retain my self-possession, that I betrayed not in the least a feeling which I am not at all ashamed to say amounted to positive agony.

"Mrs. Markles burst into tears, and hid her face. Assured now that she was acting a part assigned to her in a vile plot probably against my life, I could scarcely refrain from a furious outbreak, and thereby ending the scene. If I had thus ended the scene, my life would have ended with it.

"Another discovery. Twang went my luckless nerves once more. As I sat, my elbow rested on a wooden slab. I moved something, and turning to stop its fall, I discovered a small pistol! The woman, looking up, saw me take the pistol in my hand. In an instant she started up, and snatched it from me.

" ' Oh, sir,' she said, ' I am so sorry you've seen that. That belongs to Joe—my poor Joe. Oh my poor husband! What will become of him!' and again there came a flood of tears.

" I held dreadfully quick counsel in my mind, whether I had not better recover the pistol by a rapid dash, fire at the curtain, and rush out of the cottage. But during the struggle, short as it might be, that concealed villain would inevitably fire at me. No, I must try something else—but what? How much longer had I to live?

" I turned to the wretched woman. Miserable accomplice as she was, I felt sorry for her even then. My regard for those who had had regard for her moved me.

" ' Mrs. Markles,' I was beginning in a solemn tone, when she suddenly rose to her feet, and burst into a scream of laughter.

" ' There,' she cried, " there, you old fool, no more. I have had my game—no more preaching or praying, except you offer up prayer *on your own* account. The idea of my being talked to! But I certainly did it well, didn't I?'

" This is the finish, I thought. My life at five minutes' purchase! It is not worth one minute now. But I will die in performance of a good action.

" ' Sarah Markles,' I said, as solemnly as I could, ' on my own account, indeed, I may well offer up prayers, but at this moment my prayer is for you. I know your past history, Sarah Markles. I know those who fondled

you when you were destitute, supported and protected
you, even to a recent date. Ah, Sarah Markles, if they
but saw you now.'

" A great change came over her face. She placed a
hand on each of my shoulders, and gazed at me earnestly—

" ' Who do you know, who do you mean ? You don't
mean Mrs. Waley and Miss Martha Sands, do you ?'

" ' Yes I do. They are my relatives. They have
written me all about you.'

" She staggered back, her hands before her eyes.

" ' Are you not sorry to have left them ?'

" ' Sorry !' she almost screamed (and what a tale of
suffering and of, at all events, temporary remorse, her
face revealed at that moment !) ' but,' she said hurriedly, ' no more of that now. You say Mrs. Waley
and Miss Martha Sands are your relatives ; what relatives ?'

" ' Mrs. Waley is my grandmother. Miss Martha
Sands is my niece.'

" Again she placed her hands before her eyes, and some
low muttering escaped her, in which I could distinguish
the word ' never ' twice repeated. When she withdrew her hand, I was aghast, so awfully pale she looked.
I had taken my hat, and was about placing it on my
head, when, with a loud scream, she snatched it from me.
At that moment the cloth was pulled furiously down,
a pistol was discharged, a horrid yell arose, and a heavy
body rolled into the centre of the room. Appalled and

scared, I was momentarily paralysed. But I saw the prostrate body was that of Joe Markles, and the discharged pistol was not in his hand, but in that of his wife. She had shot him down in his hiding place, just as he was springing from it. And my conviction was then, and is now, that she killed him as the only means of saving my life.

"Yet for an instant she seemed to regret the deed.

"'I have done it!—I have done it!' she screamed. 'Oh, that it should have come to this!'

"Another pistol shot shook the building. Another awful dying cry; another form writhing on the floor. My very brain reeled. The last thought of the expiring husband was revenge on his wretched wife, the last movement was its execution. He had clutched again a pistol which had fallen from him when he received his death-wound, and on that blood-stained floor husband and wife lay together dead.

"The moon had risen ere I left the cottage. I must have been insensible for some time. I cast a shuddering look at two still figures lying close together, then hurried forth."

THE END.

Lightning Source UK Ltd.
Milton Keynes UK
UKHW020639171022
410608UK00009B/579